The SEARCH for GOD'S OWN HEART

The SEARCH for GOD'S OWN HEART

Finding a Genuine Relationship with God

ANDY COOK

kregel
PUBLICATIONS

Grand Rapids, MI 49501

The Search for God's Own Heart: Finding a Genuine Relationship with God

© 2001 by Andy Cook

Published by Kregel Publications, a division of Kregel, Inc., P.O. Box 2607, Grand Rapids, MI 49501. For more information about Kregel Publications, visit our web site: www.kregel.com.

Cover design: John M. Lucas

Library of Congress Cataloging-in-Publication Data
Cook, Andy.
    The search for God's own heart: finding a genuine relationship with God / Andy Cook.
        p.   cm.
Includes bibliographical references.
    1. Bible. O.T. Samuel—Criticism, interpretation, etc. 2. God—Knowableness. I. Title.
BS1325.52 .C66   2001   248.4—dc21   2001023033
                                                                          CIP
ISBN 0-8254-2389-9

Printed in the United States of America

1 2 3 4 5 / 05 04 03 02 01

Contents

Foreword

I have known Andy Cook for many years and have followed his ministry with great anticipation and expectation. I first knew him as a member of Bellevue Baptist Church, where I have served as pastor for twenty-seven years.

I watched Andy grow in the Lord and was blessed to be his pastor when he and his lovely wife, Melody, surrendered to God's call to the ministry. Without a moment's hesitation, he sold his home in Lake Wildwood, resigned as sports editor of *The Macon Telegraph*, and enrolled at Southeastern Baptist Theological Seminary, where he earned a Master of Divinity degree. In his second year at the school, his classmates honored him by choosing him to be one of just three student speakers at chapel. God has honored his ministry in both North Carolina and Georgia.

This, his first book, contains a powerful, honest, and forthright presentation of humankind's search to find a genuine relationship with God. Andy's introductory confession of a simple, careless act that resulted in a lost pitchfork, and the havoc it could have produced, stabs at the very heart of our problem—the desire to shun responsibility for our sins. This book traces this defect of humankind through the Old Testament with an accurate, truthful, and in-depth study of David's search for the right road and a right relationship with God. As you read these pages, you will often find yourself in the position of prayer. I know I did!

This book will capture your attention, from the introduction to the very last page. You will find yourself laughing at some of the situations and praising God for His intervention and answers to prayer. The end result could be a stronger faith and a genuine relationship with God. To arrive there, all of us must travel the road of genuine repentance and complete honesty with God.

It is my earnest belief that, if you are honestly seeking God's heart, you can find it here. Let the search begin!

—DR. NEAL WALL
Pastor, Bellevue Baptist Church
Macon, Georgia

Acknowledgments

Sometimes it takes a woman brave enough to take your face in her hands, look you in the eye, and tell you what to do.

It was an emotional May afternoon when Jacquelyn Smith held me still, made me look her in the eye and listen to her heart. "You've got to promise me," she said, "that you're going to write a book." There was silence for a moment. In a few hours, we would be moving to another community, and I wouldn't be just a short walk away from this woman who had loved my family so much. "Promise," demanded the woman with tears in her eyes. There would be no compromise, and there was passion in the request. What else could I say?

"I promise."

Today, for better or worse, the promise is fulfilled.

I don't suppose I'd be at this point in life without the enormous help of those who—like Jacquelyn—have been men and women after God's own heart.

People like the folks at Bellevue Baptist Church in Macon, Georgia. They were the ones who loved us through the greatest crisis of our lives, and they birthed us into full-time ministry. Bellevue was one of many churches that had a profound influence on me. Thanks also to the Georgia churches of my childhood and earliest years of adulthood—First Baptist Church in Americus, West Highland and Vineville Baptist churches in Macon, and Beech Haven Baptist Church in Athens.

How could I have gotten here without the wonderful people at Cedar Rock First Baptist Church? Hidden away in the tobacco fields of eastern North Carolina, this church family gave me my first opportunity to be a pastor. What a risk they took!

So much of my personal growth came at First Baptist Church in Soperton, Georgia. What a blessing to be in the heart of "Million Pines" country with a church family that poured out its love on us. It was there that God also gave me a great brother in the Lord, Kent Miller—truly a man after God's own heart.

Now God has brought me to Shirley Hills Baptist Church in Warner Robins, Georgia, a church willing to build Bethlehem, if it must, in order to reach its community for Christ. Our staff has been a supportive team of men and women committed to the search for God's heart. Thanks especially to Gary Aikens, Jeff Glenn, and Ed Lycett. What an exciting future lies in front of us all!

You hold in your hands a book that would not have been possible without the work of many people. A brief but heartfelt word of thanks to those who read, edited, gave suggestions, and gave me time to write. Thanks to them all—including Brenda Brown, Tim Martin, Dr. Neal Wall (my pastor), Ann Peterson, and Mike Wehner. Thanks also to Celia Walton, Jackie Bailey, and Connie Freeman (secretaries after God's own heart!), and our entire ministry staff and church family at Shirley Hills.

Of all the study that helped me in my own study of 1 and 2 Samuel, I owe a special thanks to two writers. Beth Moore wrote the tremendous Bible study *A Heart Like His*,[1] and Charles Swindoll's *David* was as insightful as his brilliant work usually is.[2]

Of course, there is my family to thank. I have a debt of gratitude that can never be repaid to my parents, Hal and Hulda Cook, and to my "second set" of parents, Rex and Melrose Evans. God has allowed me the thrill of being father to Summer, Melinda, and Courtney, and the honor of being married to Melody for the last two decades. How can one man be surrounded by so many people who've made the search for God's heart their top priority in life?

Finally, thanks for taking the time to read these pages. To have you read this book is an honor! I pray you'll find something new about God, about God's Word, and about yourself. Thanks for caring enough about The Search to search these pages.

The Search Begins

With only a little trouble, I could take you to some of the places where The Search began for me in earnest. I would take a short drive to the other side of Asheville, North Carolina, where thick rows of mountains lean upon each other as they fill the Appalachian sky. Many summers ago, it was a majestic scene for a boy from the flatlands of Middle Georgia, and it looked like a place where someone might find a few answers to life's questions.

I had several questions for God.

At eighteen, there was a lot going on down in the valley. College was already in progress. An unfocused career was three years away. Eight hours away from the mountains was a young woman who might be the wife of my lifetime. These were important questions. The questions of my future were as routine, as familiar, and as important as your questions.

And so I went to the top of the mountains, over and over again. I climbed the peaks during the morning, the afternoon, and at night. God didn't post office hours, so I looked for Him every hour of the day.

How I hoped God would break His tradition and His silence and lay out a plan for me. I wanted a blueprint I could read, a road map I could understand, or a voice I could hear. I was sure I was ready to follow God's map—if only He would show it to me. Although I didn't know how to put it into words, it was, in biblical language, a search for God's own heart.

Nevertheless, at the time, it seemed to be a fruitless search. On top of that mountain, listening for the answers, God was as silent as the stars. He wasn't as distant as the stars, just silent.

As frustrating as it was, I was learning some difficult truths about my Maker. God *can be found,* but the search may take an entire lifetime. God *can be heard,* but His voice is so quiet, silence and stillness are the only entrances into His chamber. You *can find direction for life,* but the journey is difficult. And at the heart of the matter is *your* heart.

This frustrating search is nothing new. Centuries ago, another young man asked the same God for direction in his life. His story has inspired countless millions. He was trapped in a going-nowhere job, watching livestock on the top of another mountain, a mountain literally half a world away from my rows of mountains in North Carolina. Eventually, that young man's life would be the stuff of great drama. By the time he was a middle-aged adult, he would be recognized as a national hero and a world leader. He would marry well, find wealth, and become the most admired man of his generation. Centuries after his death, David is still one of the most admired men in all history. But at the very beginning, when he was looking hard for the answers to life, the teenaged David found the same truth that perhaps you have found. God wasn't going to give him a step-by-step plan for his life. The journey would be full of difficulties, surprises, and uncertainties.

To make matters worse, David would make a world of mistakes and literally prevent some of the blessings God had planned for him. By the end of David's lifelong search, a painful period of repentance brought him back, full circle, to the quiet contentment of searching for God's heart.

But never forget the faith in the beginning of The Search. It's almost too simple. When God's answers were still a lifetime away, David was simply a teenager searching for God's will. Ironically, this search for God's heart made David a rare find. Even today, people who honestly and desperately seek God's direction are few and far between. As it is today, it was then. As young David searched, his heart was changed. Before the boy knew what had happened, God had found a king amidst all the sheep. The reason for the honor? David's heart had been looking for God.

That's it.

That's all.

On the application form for king, God wasn't asking for anything that we'd normally ask for in a leader. No pedigree, no law degree, no money. Nevertheless, God had His man.

Isn't it strange? God had been looking for someone who would simply search for Him!

The famous biblical words that set David apart were being said while David was still a teenager, still going through the pure, simple process of asking God for direction and of waiting on God to answer. At the time, he had no inkling that a royal future was in front of him. David never could have dreamed all that God had planned for him. He would have been stunned to know that *he* was the subject of a private, world-changing conversation in a place not very far away from his sheep-covered mountain.

"The LORD has sought out a man after his own heart," said the nation's preacher to an unrepentant king, a king named Saul (1 Sam. 13:14). The "man" after God's heart was still just a boy. But sure enough, within a few years, David was a world-famous king and a man who would be forever known as a man after God's own heart.

It was a rags-to-riches, shepherd-boy-to-king story. Reading the history, it seems to have happened so very, very quickly.

But let me tell you something you already know. When it's your life and not ancient history, the process seems a lot slower.

A *lot* slower! When you're on the mountainside of the questions listening to a silent God, The Search can be agonizingly difficult.

So here we are, on the mountains of life, where this quest for God's heart continues.

You search.

I search.

We long for a road map that will give us the details of the journey, warn us of dangers and pitfalls, and tell us the best path and the best outcome for our lives. Instinctively, we know that God has the answers, so we search for God's own heart.

We also know that God's heart—and God's plan for our lives—is hard to find. The future stays focused on a blurry, foggy point in the distance. At best, like David, you and I may get to glimpse part of the road map for short periods of time. But never will we see the whole plan. Perhaps, at the end of our lives, we will look back on our journeys and see how God mapped it all out. But today, at this very moment, the future won't come into complete focus. By God's deliberate design, all we can really do at the beginning is find the faith to start traveling down an uncertain path.

Frankly, that's the beauty of looking back at another life, of learning from another time in history. The three-thousand-year-old lessons of David, of a king named Saul, of a preacher named Samuel, of a group of people from another time, can give us an amazingly focused, crystal-clear look at our own path, our own journey. We can take the stories of David and the people around him and learn great lessons for our own lives.

If you're longing for a genuine relationship with God, read on. If you're approaching an important crossroad of life, read on. If you long for God to break His silence and show you part of the road map for your life, read on. In one way, this book is about the people you'll find in two Bible books, 1 and 2 Samuel. But in another way, these ancient stories are actually about us. Like the people you'll meet in Samuel's books, you and I have a simple choice to make. We all make intentional decisions either to be—or not be—people searching for the very heart of God.

I'm glad we can travel this journey together.

Our journey is made up of countless roads, innumerable options from which we must choose. But right in front of us is the one major highway every person must travel on the journey toward God's own heart. This highway is unavoidable if we really want to find what we're looking for. We can't take shortcuts, and we can't find another way. It's this way or no way at all.

And believe it or not, this highway, this road to God's heart, is just as real as the asphalt road where the pitchfork fell not very long ago. The pitchfork? You will read about it next!

CHAPTER 1

The Road of Repentance

It was a borrowed truck and a borrowed pitchfork. The turn was made a bit too quickly, and the pitchfork slid silently across the open tailgate and landed squarely in the middle of traffic.

From the rearview mirror, I could see the cars swerving into the oncoming lane of traffic, and I could see the string of brake lights marking the state of emergency. It was another few seconds before the truth hit me. Some idiot had dropped a pitchfork on the road, and that idiot was me!

I almost continued on the journey, hoping the cars behind me had stopped because of another's boneheadedness. Had it not been a borrowed pitchfork, maybe I would have left it there, a price paid for a stupid mistake.

But I couldn't just leave it there, so I circled the block and returned to the scene of the crime.

By the time I pulled up to the stop sign, traffic on the busy road was back to normal. There was no carnage visible. I could see safety had been restored because two of the drivers had stopped in order to remove the hazard. A nice-looking man and a kind-faced woman were on the side of the road. They had been eyewitnesses to "the fall," and the man stuck the fork in the ground with a force that showed his disdain for the pick-up cowboy who'd done the deed. They were obviously talking about the close call on the busy street, shaking their heads at careless drivers like me, and trying to return to their schedules. The borrowed trouble was stuck in the ground, just thirty feet away. The broken handle was standing naked and exposed, waiting on the idiot to return. I watched it all, unnoticed, from the stop sign just a few steps away.

"If they'd only leave," I thought. "If they'd only walk away, I'd grab that fork and run. No one would know."

They didn't leave quickly enough, and the traffic behind me was pushing me to make a decision. Turn right, and I could go right past Mr. and Ms. Safety, and they'd spot me. Turn right, and I'd have to apologize and sheepishly reclaim the instrument of my wrongdoing. Turn right, and I might have to pay for damage done, though I could see no damage. Turn right, and I'd certainly have to endure a lecture.

The car behind demanded a decision.

I turned left.

I took the long way across town and hoped the pitchfork would be there later, when no one would know the story of the man who forgets to close tailgates. Hours later, it was still there. Under the cover of darkness, I reclaimed my forked failure.

I was also left with some questions I didn't want to answer. What in the world made a usually reasonable man turn away from an opportunity to be corrected? What could have brought me back under the cover of darkness to undo any sign of daylight weakness?

More than likely, you know what made me act irrationally. It's something deep inside us that tells us to take any road—*any road*—other than the Road of Repentance.

If you are searching for God's own heart, let me promise you something. You will never, ever find God apart from the Road of Repentance. Study the pavement, find the dividing lines, and read the map well. The only way to finish—to even begin—this journey is to get on the right highway.

A King Who Couldn't Find the Right Road

Samuel's age-old story of two kings is an amazing illustration of the contrasting personalities in our own lives. One personality in each of us seeks to be a king like Saul, never repenting of what we've done wrong. The other personality, the one after God's own heart, will fall on its knees beside David and search for God through repentance.

Don't miss this truth. Right off the bat, this Road of Repentance is as real, as important, as vital to your search for God as any other factor. There is no other road that will take you to God's heart. Miss this truth, and you'll miss God.

Saul, King Saul, tried to find happiness in other ways. Consider, for a moment, the story of his life. Saul was chosen as king, by God, through the prophet Samuel. Here was a young man who had it all together. The Bible describes him as "an impressive young man without equal among the Israelites—a head taller than any of the others."

We would have called him the star quarterback for the high school football team. We would have seen the headlines proclaiming his talent, his future, his charisma. His school yearbook would have labeled him "Most Likely to Succeed." The picture of him would have included half a dozen young ladies in the background, hoping to catch his eye—a sparkling, winking eye.

Saul had it all, and his dad was loaded. While David's dad raised sheep, Saul's dad raised donkeys.

In Israel some three thousand years ago, donkeys were luxuries. It was as if Saul's dad had the Mercedes dealership in Central Israel. As a teenager, Saul was the detail man, getting the donkeys ready for sale, riding new, dealership donkeys to school every morning, flashing his family's money in front of the student body.

In a short time, Saul was king. He was tabbed by Samuel, approved by the people, and most importantly, he was chosen by God. "Do whatever your hand finds to do," Samuel told the young man, "for *God is with you*" (1 Sam. 10:7, emphasis added).

Think about it. A blank check from God!

Despite Saul's fear and insecurities, he really did become his nation's leader. A battle was quickly held and quickly won. And at his inauguration celebration, some internal enemies were found, arrested, and lined up for execution.

> The people then said to Samuel, "Who was it that asked, 'Shall Saul reign over us?' Bring these men to us and we will put them to death."
>
> But Saul said, "No one shall be put to death today, for this day the LORD has rescued Israel."
>
> Then Samuel said to the people, "Come, let us go to Gilgal and there reaffirm the kingship." So all the people went to Gilgal and confirmed Saul as king in the presence of the LORD. There they sacrificed fellowship offerings before the LORD, and Saul and all the Israelites held a great celebration.
>
> —1 Samuel 11:12–15

Unfortunately, Saul's first day in office was also his finest day. It wouldn't be long before the pitchfork would fall out of the truck, and Saul would spend nearly the rest of his life turning left, avoiding the Road of Repentance.

Early in his forty-two-year reign as king, Saul came to a tougher battle. The Philistines had an army that couldn't be numbered, and Saul's troops were shaking in their boots. This wasn't just any terrified army; this was God's army. Saul was God's leader for God's army, and this was an emergency situation. The crisis was at hand.

Standard procedure for God's army included worship. The soldiers had heard stories of God's provision, of battlefield miracles, of a fighting God. And as they should have, they built an altar, held a lamb, and waited on the preacher.

Perhaps Samuel, the preacher of the day, was delayed. Perhaps some of the roads were closed because of the battle. Perhaps the prophet waited on purpose. Perhaps God detained Samuel, waiting to see what kind of heart His new king had. It happens that way, you know.

> Saul remained at Gilgal, and all the troops with him were quaking with fear. He waited seven days, the time set by Samuel; but Samuel did not come to Gilgal, and Saul's men began to scatter. So he said, "Bring me the burnt offering and the fellowship offerings." And Saul offered up the burnt offering. Just as he finished making the offering, Samuel arrived, and Saul went out to greet him.
>
> "What have you done?" asked Samuel.
>
> Saul replied, "When I saw that the men were scattering, and that you did not come at the set time, and that the Philistines were assembling at Micmash, I thought, 'Now the Philistines will come down against me at Gilgal, and I have not sought the LORD's favor.' So I felt compelled to offer the burnt offering."
>
> "You acted foolishly," Samuel said. "You have not kept the command the LORD your God gave you; if you had, he would have established your kingdom over Israel for all time. But now your kingdom will not endure; the LORD has sought out a man after his own heart and appointed him leader of his people, because you have not kept the LORD's command."
>
> Then Samuel left Gilgal and went up to Gibeah in Benjamin, and Saul counted the men who were with him. They numbered about six hundred.
>
> —1 Samuel 13:7–15

Did you see the left turn? Read the rest of the Bible if you like, but you will never find Saul repenting for what he had done in his tight spot. He rationalized it in his mind, he was embarrassed, and he was angry at a prophet's correction. After all, it was the prophet who was late. Didn't this preacher know that the nation's security was at stake? When the preacher didn't show, and the time for battle was waning away, Saul took matters into his own hands. He had done what he thought was best. He was the right man, in the right place, in the right position, but he had done the wrong thing in the wrong way. The pitchfork was bouncing around the pavement.

Saul would not, absolutely would not, say that he had made a mistake.

But he *had* made a mistake. He had stepped deliberately into an area that he knew wasn't his.

After the sin, like all of us, Saul had an opportunity to take the Road of Repentance. Saul didn't repent. If he had been searching for God, he soon found that God wouldn't give His presence, or His deliverance, to an unrepentant heart. There would be no miracle for this king. When he counted his troops, he found six hundred unarmed, trembling soldiers. This military scenario was bad news, but the worst news was in the king's heart. He had chosen a highway other than the narrow, difficult Road of Repentance.

The pattern would hold true for the rest of Saul's career. He took his own path. He ignored the things of God. Like a Sunday school teacher, like a deacon, like a pastor, he held the right title, he dressed the right way, he went through the right motions. But his heart was growing increasingly hollow. He was having more and more trouble hearing God's correction.

As the years grew into decades, God gave Saul many, many second chances. Like a lot of us, Saul had *years* of second chances.

Eventually, the day came when the second chances ended. In another battle, with a better army, Saul faced the Amalekites. Through the voice of Samuel, God had instructed Saul to take the victory, and Saul went. The battle was begun.

In this battle, Saul's main instruction from God was to completely destroy every living man, woman, child, cow, horse, chicken, and donkey—*every* creature in that city. There was no doubting the instruction. It was as clear as the instructions you read in the Bible for your life.

On this day, God gave Saul the victory. Following the king's orders, Saul's men put every person in that city to death, except one. Saul decided to keep the king alive. On top of that, some of the men pointed out that the animals in the city would be good payment for the war. They were valuable spoils of victory. Saul agreed, and the best animals were kept alive. It was a great move for Saul, the politician. A chicken in every pot, a heifer in every barn! In the thrill of victory—in the wake of God's victory—Saul even allowed some of the men to erect a monument to him, the victorious king (see 1 Sam. 15:12).

Were it not so serious a matter, the scene that followed would be comical.

Picture, for a moment, the great caravan of animals and soldiers, returning home in triumph. Coming over the horizon is a prophet, the man with the original word from God. Samuel was the man who had heard God's Spirit command: Kill *every living creature* in the city.

Samuel—one man on the horizon—sees the army of hundreds on the opposite horizon. The two sides are on a collision course. Saul's men are drunk with victory, herding livestock won in the lottery of life. The captured king is paraded in front of the rowdy band, a trophy to be kept alive for years of enjoyment. It is a noisy group, Saul's band of winners.

When Saul sees the prophet, he quickly decides to ignore the disobedience. He puts a new spin on the day. With his hand caught in the cookie jar, he smiles at his mother and says, "Hey Mom, great cookies! Wouldn't you like one?"

Samuel didn't return the smile. Instead, he confronts the creative lying. Here's the story:

> When Samuel reached him, Saul said, "The LORD bless you! *I have carried out the Lord's instructions.*"
>
> But Samuel said, "What then is this bleating of sheep in my ears? What is this lowing of cattle that I hear?"
>
> Saul answered, "The *soldiers brought them* from the Amalekites; they spared the best of the sheep and cattle *to sacrifice to the Lord your God,* but we totally destroyed the rest."
>
> —1 Samuel 15:13–15, emphasis added

Did you see all the lies? Saul said he had carried out the Lord's instructions. He hadn't. Saul said it was the soldiers who had done the wrong thing. Perhaps they had, but they had done so with Saul's permission. It was his fault, not their sin. And what gall this man had—"We're saving these animals to sacrifice them. They're an offering to God, Samuel!" The animals were an offering to individual checkbooks, a reward given for fighting well. And finally, a telling comment: "Samuel, we're going to give them to the Lord *your* God." Isn't that something? From his heart, Saul speaks, and from his heart, he cannot speak of "the Lord *my* God." Disobedience had led to lying, and a lifetime of non-repentance had killed Saul's personal relationship with a loving God. There was nothing genuine about Saul's walk with God. Now he would suffer greatly. Here the story continues:

"Stop!" Samuel said to Saul. "Let me tell you what the Lord said to me last night."

"Tell me," Saul replied.

Samuel said, "Although you were once small in your own eyes, did you not become the head of the tribes of Israel? The Lord anointed you king over Israel. And he sent you on a mission, saying, 'Go and completely destroy those wicked people, the Amalekites; make war on them until you have wiped them out.' Why did you not obey the Lord? Why did you pounce on the plunder and do evil in the eyes of the Lord?"

"But I did obey the Lord," Saul said. "I went on the mission the Lord assigned me. I completely destroyed the Amalekites and brought back Agag their king. The soldiers took sheep and cattle from the plunder, the best of what was devoted to God, in order to sacrifice them to the Lord your God at Gilgal."

But Samuel replied:

"Does the Lord delight in burnt offerings and sacrifices as much as in obeying the voice of the Lord?

To obey is better than sacrifice,
　　and to heed is better than the fat of rams.
For rebellion is like the sin of divination,
　　and arrogance like the evil of idolatry.
Because you have rejected the word of the LORD,
　　he has rejected you as king."

　　　　　　　　　　　　　　　　—1 Samuel 15:16–23

Now watch this. It's hard to see, but here is a glimpse at the heart of a man who is *not* a man after God's heart:

> Then Saul said to Samuel, "I have sinned. I violated the LORD's command and your instructions. I was afraid of the people and so I gave in to them. Now I beg you, forgive my sin and come back with me, so that I may worship the LORD."
>
> But Samuel said to him, "I will not go back with you. You have rejected the word of the LORD, and the LORD has rejected you as king over Israel!"
>
> As Samuel turned to leave, Saul caught hold of the hem of his robe, and it tore. Samuel said to him, "The LORD has torn the kingdom of Israel from you today and has given it to one of your neighbors—to one better than you. He who is the Glory of Israel does not lie or change his mind; for he is not a man, that he should change his mind."
>
> 　　　　　　　　　　　　　　　　—1 Samuel 15:24–29

Did you see it? Saul had not sinned against Samuel, he had sinned against God. He had violated clear orders and then tried to dress the sin up as something he had done for God! But now, he was caught red-handed. Though Saul could see the pitchfork stuck alongside the road, ready to be claimed, he turned left, again. He chose to not repent of his sin to God. Look at the verses again, for they are important. Saul, the man not after God's heart, would talk *about* God, but he would not talk *to* God.

By the end of this day, Samuel did return with Saul, and Saul did worship the Lord. After the worship, Saul still didn't make things right with God, for it was Samuel who had to have the enemy king put to death. Repentance isn't just being sorry for something done wrong. Repentance includes taking action to make things right. Saul simply couldn't—or wouldn't—take that action.

At the heart of the matter, the king had a heart problem. Saul had suffered from this spiritual defect in his youth, and it followed him into adulthood. By his own choosing, Saul never had been a man after God's own heart.

From that day forward, Samuel, the mentor, the pastor, grieved for Saul, the disobedient king. He would never see Saul again. Saul's failure hurt the old prophet deeply. As a young man, Saul had started with so much promise. But as life progressed, Saul simply could not force himself to travel the Road of Repentance.

Saul would live out the rest of his life in a heart-breaking, pathetic, downward spiral. In the last few days of his life, he would seek help from a five-dollar palmist and beg a child to take his life. When the child wouldn't obey, Saul fell on his sword, and his life was over.

A King Who Knew the Road of Repentance

There is, of course, another king in the story. David was the teenaged hero, the boy who would lead his country. It was years before he would actually redecorate the throne room, but David was kingly material right from the start.

No, he wasn't as handsome as Saul. If Saul was the all-star quarterback, David was the hidden left guard, the one rarely seen by the fans, the coaches, or the scouts. Not even Samuel was able to pick him out of the crowd as a future leader.

Still, the kid was a king. The evidence wasn't on the outside, it was on the inside.

> The LORD said to Samuel, "Do not consider his appearance or his height. . . . The LORD does not look at the

things man looks at. Man looks at the outward appearance, but the LORD looks at the heart."

—1 Samuel 16:7

God knew the truth: David's heart was already searching for God.

There would be another preacher who would confront David's sin, many years and many sins down the road. The sins confronted were every bit as serious as the ones Saul had dropped in the middle of the road. How serious? Try adultery, and then add murder. There was a cover-up and a bed made of lies. There was a drawing away from God, and the entire kingdom knew of the misdeeds. Probably, all over the country, people were following their compromised leader with compromises of their own. Samuel was dead, so it was a preacher named Nathan who came into David's throne room with "news" from the countryside. Actually, the preacher only had a story. And the story, David soon saw, was about him. He saw it with the clarity of Nathan's cut-to-the-point application.

> The LORD sent Nathan to David. When he came to him, he said, "There were two men in a certain town, one rich and the other poor. The rich man had a very large number of sheep and cattle, but the poor man had nothing except one little ewe lamb he had bought. He raised it, and it grew up with him and his children. It shared his food, drank from his cup and even slept in his arms. It was like a daughter to him.
>
> "Now a traveler came to the rich man, but the rich man refrained from taking one of his own sheep or cattle to prepare a meal for the traveler who had come to him. Instead, he took the ewe lamb that belonged to the poor man and prepared it for the one who had come to him."
>
> David burned with anger against the man and said to Nathan, "As surely as the LORD lives, the man who did this deserves to die! He must pay for that lamb four

times over, because he did such a thing and had no
pity."

Then Nathan said to David, "You are the man!" . . .

Then David said to Nathan, "I have sinned against
the LORD."

—2 Samuel 12:1–7, 13

There it is. Immediately, suddenly, David looks his sin squarely
in the face and says, "I'm sorry; I'm wrong." His actions confirmed what we couldn't have seen with our eyes. Now we can see
what was in his heart. Unlike Saul, David took action. His broken,
repentant heart forced some real-life decisions. David began a
fast that lasted seven days. David prayed for his child's life, the
child born to Uriah's wife, the child of David's wrongdoing. He
spent his nights, not in the feathered bed of seduction, but on the
ground, on the dirt Road of Repentance. And when the son died,
David got up, washed, put on fresh clothes, and headed for the
temple. Before he would feed his body, he would feed his soul.
He would worship the King of Kings.

Can you see the contrast with Saul's life? A man after God's
own heart had to cleanse his own heart before he could find God
again. The road to the temple was the rocky Road of Repentance.
There was no other path, no other highway, no other direction.

Centuries later, there still has never been built a new road that
leads to God's heart. Even at the beginning of the search for a
genuine, life-changing relationship with God, one thing is painfully clear. A man or woman seeking God's heart is not going to
find God in his or her efforts at perfection. It's impossible. All of
us, like Saul, like David, have done things that are clearly wrong.
But a person after God's own heart is the person willing to face
his or her own sin and say to God, "I'm sorry. I shouldn't have
done that. Please forgive me."

And as simply as that, God is found on the Road of Repentance.

You know, a man after God's own heart *must* learn how to turn
back, face the music, and pick up the broken pitchfork.

CHAPTER 2

A Choice of Two Ebenezers

Maybe you've heard the story of the cowboy out West who was driving down a dirt road, his dog riding in back of the pickup truck, his faithful horse in the trailer behind. The cowboy failed to negotiate a curve and had a terrible accident.

Sometime later, a highway patrol officer came on the scene. He saw the horse first. Realizing the serious nature of its injuries, he drew his service revolver and put the animal out of his misery. He walked around the accident and found the dog, also critically hurt. He couldn't bear to hear it whine in pain, so he ended the dog's suffering as well. Finally, off in the weeds, he located the cowboy, who had suffered multiple injuries. A broken arm, a twisted leg, bruises inside and out. "Hey, are you OK?" the officer asked.

The cowboy took one look at the smoking revolver in the trooper's hand and quickly replied, "Never felt better!"

In order to live, that old cowboy faked it.

If you want to live with God, don't fake it.

One of the most important messages we can hear today is the

simple message that we must not fake it with God. Let me cut to the core. Holding fast to a *religion* is faking it. Having a *relationship* with the Living God is the real thing. You can have all the trappings of ritual, tradition, social standing, or even a years-long membership in a church. But what God wants is something entirely different. God desires for us to have a relationship with Him.

The Bible offers us today a choice of two "Ebenezers." Two different places, two different events. Two different ways to relate to God, two different lifestyles as God's people. They're as different as night and day, as starkly different as horrible defeat and great, marvelous victory.

We start with the Bible's report of a horrible defeat and finish with the Bible's report of a great victory. The two events were twenty years apart, in places about twenty miles apart. Both events, however, include a name that is very, very prominent in the stories— the name of Ebenezer. The name means "Stone of Help." It is a name referring to God's ability and power to help His people.

The first Ebenezer was a village. Before we read about the event that took place just outside Ebenezer, use your imagination a little. Paint the picture, if you will, of the first Ebenezer. I think it was a sleepy little community. A few farmers, a few shepherds, a bakery, and a general store with a tree-lined boulevard in the heart of town. Not much to this Ebenezer, until the day the army came to town. Thousands and thousands of soldiers started coming, and they camped in the fields of Ebenezer. Before this battle was over, thirty-four thousand Israelites were dead, so the number of people gathered in the little village must have been overwhelming.

It was heady stuff for the townsfolk. They were famous, and they were gaining a reputation. And then there was that brief, giddy, ecstatic moment for the local chamber of commerce when the ark of the covenant came through town. The ark was the most sacred piece of furniture ever built. Ebenezer, they knew, would never be the same.

They were right, of course, and dead wrong, both at the same time. Try to imagine what a nightmare it was when God didn't help the people of Ebenezer.

Now the Israelites went out to fight against the Philistines. The Israelites camped at Ebenezer, and the Philistines at Aphek. The Philistines deployed their forces to meet Israel, and as the battle spread, Israel was defeated by the Philistines, who killed about four thousand of them on the battlefield. When the soldiers returned to camp, the elders of Israel asked, "Why did the Lord bring defeat upon us today before the Philistines? Let us bring the ark of the Lord's covenant from Shiloh, so that it may go with us and save us from the hand of our enemies."

So the people sent men to Shiloh, and they brought back the ark of the covenant of the Lord Almighty, who is enthroned between the cherubim. And Eli's two sons, Hophni and Phinehas, were there with the ark of the covenant of God.

When the ark of the Lord's covenant came into the camp, all Israel raised such a great shout that the ground shook. Hearing the uproar, the Philistines asked, "What's all this shouting in the Hebrew camp?"

When they learned that the ark of the Lord had come into the camp, the Philistines were afraid. "A god has come into the camp," they said. "We're in trouble! Nothing like this has happened before. Woe to us! Who will deliver us from the hand of these mighty gods? They are the gods who struck the Egyptians with all kinds of plagues in the desert. Be strong, Philistines! Be men, or you will be subject to the Hebrews, as they have been to you. Be men, and fight!"

So the Philistines fought, and the Israelites were defeated and every man fled to his tent. The slaughter was very great; Israel lost thirty thousand foot soldiers. The ark of God was captured, and Eli's two sons, Hophni and Phinehas, died.

—1 Samuel 4:1–11

For the Israelites, nothing worse could have happened than to have lost the ark of the covenant. As it turns out, nothing worse could have happened to the Philistines, either! The ark became a curse to the Philistines. Before long, they asked the Israelites to take it back and to remove from them the curses, and the people of God gladly received it. However, there was still disaster and defeat all around. For starters, thirty-four thousand soldiers were dead. In addition, the Philistines had invaded and taken over entire villages and communities. The national border of Israel had been pushed back toward Jerusalem by at least twenty miles.

After twenty years pass, we find the Israelites under Samuel's leadership—not Eli's rule—as they gather at a place called Mizpah. After two decades of suffering, the Israelites have no military might, and they have no confidence in themselves. But these people do believe that they will be rescued by the hand of God, their spiritual Ebenezer, their "stone of help."

> When the Philistines heard that Israel had assembled at Mizpah, the rulers of the Philistines came up to attack them. And when the Israelites heard of it, they were afraid because of the Philistines. They said to Samuel, "Do not stop crying out to the LORD our God for us, that he may rescue us from the hand of the Philistines." Then Samuel took a suckling lamb and offered it up as a whole burnt offering to the LORD. He cried out to the LORD on Israel's behalf, and the LORD answered him.
>
> While Samuel was sacrificing the burnt offering, the Philistines drew near to engage Israel in battle. But that day the LORD thundered with loud thunder against the Philistines and threw them into such a panic that they were routed before the Israelites. The men of Israel rushed out of Mizpah and pursued the Philistines, slaughtering them along the way to a point below Beth Car.
>
> Then Samuel took a stone and set it up between Mizpah and Shen. He named it Ebenezer, saying, "Thus

far has the LORD helped us." So the Philistines were subdued and did not invade Israelite territory again.

Throughout Samuel's lifetime, the hand of the LORD was against the Philistines.

—1 Samuel 7:7–13

The second Ebenezer was just a rock. A large rock, mind you, but just a rock. It was a stone symbol of God's miracle-working power. It was a large, rock-hard reminder that God is not moved, that God is a rock to rest upon. It was an Ebenezer of trusting God and God alone.

I'd like to invite you today not to a religion—which leads to a futile and hopeless place like the first Ebenezer—but to a relationship with the living God. It's an invitation to live near the second Ebenezer, Samuel's monument that marked God's miraculous deliverance. And really, it's not my invitation at all. It's God's invitation. It's the Bible's invitation.

The Bible is so practical, so full of truth, that we get to see real people living in real situations, people who look amazingly like you and me. Our focus of the moment is a man named Samuel.

Samuel was a prophet, a great man of God, a man who had a heart that searched for God's heart. He didn't have a religion—he had a relationship with God. He is a man worth studying, for if we can model our lives after his life, we'll be well on the way to finding God's own heart.

One thing I've learned from studying Samuel's life and these two Ebenezers is that a person who wants a relationship with God will have a healthy fear of God.

The Fear of the Lord

Right at the beginning of Proverbs, the Bible's book of wisdom statements, there is this jewel: "The fear of the LORD is the beginning of knowledge" (Prov. 1:7).

Solomon wrote the words, but he learned this from his father David, who learned it from Samuel. Samuel learned the truth of this principle, the gut-wrenching, brow-sweating side of this truth, from the experiences recorded for us in 1 Samuel 5–6, when thirty-four thousand died outside the village of Ebenezer. As we consider what happened, remember that young Samuel, perhaps still just an older child of twelve, watched that disastrous day with his own eyes! It profoundly affected him. He developed a great fear, a healthy respect, for God and the things of God.

He saw the Philistines raid the land, attack the soldiers at Ebenezer, and capture the sacred ark. Little Samuel heard how the Philistines treated the ark with gross disrespect. Then he heard the reports of what was happening to the enemies who owned what they figured was a "box of god."

They never counted on the god being God!

Do you remember the story? In the Philistine city of Ashdod, there was an outbreak of tumors for the people with the captured ark. Then a statue of the false god Dagon was mysteriously destroyed. When the ark was moved to Gath, there was another outbreak of tumors, some leading to death. Panic ensued, and the Philistines wanted to send the ark back to Israel.

Samuel began to understand that the enemies of God would do best to find a healthy fear of God. But what happened next really burned the lesson into his heart.

According to 1 Samuel 6, the ark was returned to Israel, and the people of Beth Shemesh (a town on the border) celebrated wildly. They were the first to see the ark returned, along with the gold offerings the Philistines had included with the ark to apologize for taking such a sacred thing.

Imagine the spirit of celebration that was in Beth Shemesh. Picture the dancing in the street, the wild manner of worship, the profound belief that God was, somehow, still in control.

But also picture the corner café, where a group of men, decked out in their baseball caps and drinking cups of coffee, start to relish their lofty position. It was their city, after all, that held the ark of God. The box was in their possession. God was smiling on them, and they liked the idea.

As the celebration wore off and the coffee turned cold, something else began to brew in the minds of the men at the café. When the ark was captured weeks before, they knew the hidden items on the inside were supposed to be there. They all knew—they *all* knew—that it contained the Ten Commandments, along with a jar of manna, and Aaron's rod. There was some honest worry. Were the items still there? Had the ungodly Philistines returned *everything*? Was it all in good order?

But there was something more than just a bit of sacred concern here. And remember as this story progresses, that God sees directly into the heart. He skips over the skin, the clothes, the position, the words we say, and He goes straight to the heart. What did these guys really want?

Maybe some of them wondered if the talk of the stuff in the ark was true. Was it all just a legend? Someone with an air of religious righteousness shouted: "What if the Philistines damaged the Ten Commandments?" Someone else added the logical thought that, indeed, the ark was for them to protect, for the miraculous way God had delivered it to them proved it so. In the course of a few more cups of coffee, and maybe even some stronger drink, they had talked themselves into a frenzy, and they found themselves standing over the ark. Finally, one man lifted the lid and looked inside.

Never mind that the instructions surrounding the ark had been frighteningly clear. They all knew the stories of the priests of God who died immediately for the slightest miscue around the ark. To look inside like this was asking for the wrath of God. But no, they had convinced themselves that it would be OK to bend the rules of God, since they were the children of God. Because they felt like it, they figured that God would agree to a slight changing of the rules, a momentary compromise.

They figured wrong.

> But God struck down some of the men of Beth Shemesh, putting seventy of them to death because they had looked into the ark of the LORD.
>
> —1 Samuel 6:19

Now here is an interesting picture to consider. Tumors for the Philistines, death for the Israelites. It's unbelievable: God literally punished His own children more harshly for a lesser-looking crime than He had the ungodly Philistines for crimes that seemed much more serious.

This still is true. God reacts very strongly when those of us who have taken His name as our names disobey His rules. Jesus said, according to Revelation 3:19, "Those *whom I love* I rebuke and discipline. So be earnest, and repent" (emphasis added).

From that day forward, the people of Samuel's time were much more careful with the things of God. They had seen the disaster that had fallen upon Eli's house, and now they had seen the punishment upon the men of Beth Shemesh. They were in awe of God. They were in shock. They feared God.

But what good news that is! As Proverbs 1:7 says, "The fear of the LORD is the beginning of knowledge." Now that Israel feared God, they were on the verge of an age of wisdom. Now that Samuel really understood fear, he would be able to lead in a powerful way. In just twenty years, these God-fearing people would have a great victory.

I must put this as plainly as possible. Once you choose the name of Christ, once you stand with God, all the rules change. God will hold you accountable for the things you do, the actions you take. And God will hold you *more accountable* than the people around you who are not Christians.

That highly unusual-sounding principle is true because God is constantly seeking a relationship with you. Just as God punished the Philistines with tumors but hammered the Israelites with death, God wants His own people to have a healthy fear of Him.

Do you fear the things of God? God has laid down such specific rules, such clear guidelines. Do you fear them enough to actually obey God? Or maybe the question should go back to the core of the matter. How badly do you want a relationship with God? A relationship with God demands a healthy fear of God.

I beg those of you who have taken the name of Christ, those of you who have said, "I'm a Christian," to take the lesson to heart—

God's hand of correction will fall the quickest and the heaviest upon His own children, because He loves you. The first part of having a relationship with God is simply having a healthy fear of God.

The second part of having a relationship with God is understanding the role of adversity in cultivating that relationship. Adversity is a fertile garden for the planting and nurturing of a relationship with God.

The Garden of Adversity

If you have chosen to pursue a relationship with God, you will go through some tough times and recognize, even in the midst of the adversity, that God is doing a work in your life—a work of faith. If you have tried to fake it with God by choosing ritual or religion or by taking shortcuts with faith, adversity will simply be adversity. You'll shake your fist in the face of God at the slightest sign of trouble and scream: "All of this time, wasted. God, you haven't taken care of me!"

But watch how the garden of adversity grew into a great field of faith for the people Samuel pastored. They had been beaten, terrorized, and constantly threatened by the Philistines for twenty long years. What they did at Mizpah, just a few yards down the road from Samuel's Rock of Ebenezer, is worth reading again.

> When they had assembled at Mizpah, they drew water and poured it out before the LORD. On that day they fasted and there they confessed, "We have sinned against the LORD." And Samuel was leader of Israel at Mizpah.
>
> When the Philistines heard that Israel had assembled at Mizpah, the rulers of the Philistines came up to attack them. And when the Israelites heard of it, they were afraid because of the Philistines.
>
> —1 Samuel 7:6–7

Get this into clear focus. As those folks gathered, with adversity just up the road and growing stronger by the minute, they began to fast and to confess their sins. That, in total, was their battle plan. Think about it. If they hadn't been in the midst of adversity—if they had been stronger—they would have gathered up spears and clubs and horses; they would have mapped out battle plans and met in briefing rooms; they would have operated completely in human power. And if they had owned more spears, more horses, more soldiers, they might have won. But they would have lost many lives. They would have suffered.

As it was, without the spears and horses, they could only assemble, fast, and pray. And God worked a miracle. God got down among them and changed their circumstances. God completely changed everything!

Would you like to know how you, or even an entire church, can win the battle against Satan? The same principles still apply:

1. *Assemble.* It is important to gather together. It is important, and powerful, to come together with other believers.
2. *Fast.* You can fast literally and also spiritually. Come before God with a hunger for Him. Come before God with a hunger for righteousness. Come before God with real sacrifice.
3. *Confess Sins.* Revivals start when church leaders begin confessing sins. Revival breaks out when people say: "I've been wrong. This is what I've done wrong, and I beg God's forgiveness." David said it in a song: "Against you, you only, have I sinned. . . . Create in me a pure heart, O God, and renew a steadfast spirit within me" (Ps. 51:4, 10). God can move in your life when you take down the sin barrier that you've built.

A True Relationship with God

A person with a relationship with God will talk *to* God and not just *about* God. This is such a simple thing to see, and the two Ebenezers illustrate it in blood-red color. Eli's sons, Hophni and Phinehas, both priests of God, talked about the things of God and even called for the ark of the covenant when the battle wasn't going their way at the first Ebenezer. They knew about God, they talked about God, but they had no relationship with God. As a matter of fact, they were stealing from the tabernacle offerings, they were having illicit sexual relationships with the women working at the tabernacle, and they even influenced their father to compromise his righteousness. We'll cover that soon. But for now, know this: The whole house of Eli was blatantly ungodly.

Samuel provides quite a contrast. Twenty years later, armed with a healthy fear of God, Samuel told the people about God's power, but then he went further. Samuel actually talked to God. He made a practice of having conversations with God.

Hophni and Phinehas, even as religious leaders of a nation, faked it. They talked about prayer but didn't pray. They talked about the things of God, but they didn't talk *to* God.

People still fake it today. I read about a couple whose church attendance was, well, rather lacking. The pastor of the church thought he could change that, so he asked this family to host a visiting minister for lunch. The couple obliged and put together a very special meal for the guest preacher. When they all sat down to eat, their son immediately reached for the mashed potatoes because he was used to diving right in. But since the minister was present, his mother gently stopped his hand and bowed her head in hopes he would follow her example. The boy caught on quickly. He looked around the table and saw that all of the adults were bowing their heads and closing their eyes. He was the only child present, and he wanted to impress everybody, so just as his father was about to say the blessing, the little boy belted out, "Hey Dad, can I be the one who talks to the plate?"

Samuel talked to more than the plate. He talked to God. When the battle came, Samuel's battle plan was pretty simple. He fell on his knees and on his face before God and prayed. I wonder, was he terrified? Was he confident? Was the adversity around him, the surrounding, powerful army, forcing him to admit that the only option he had was prayer?

Whatever caused Samuel to pray, the Israelites were wise enough to recognize that it was this man's prayers that were being answered by God. They believed, they trusted, and then, in amazement, they watched God intervene and defeat the Philistines for them. The only military battle of the day was when the Israelite soldiers chased the Philistines along the road that led back to the coast. Cities were recovered, and there was peace throughout the land.

Victory went back to one man praying for the nation.

The people who watched Samuel pray would agree with the apostle James, who lived centuries later. By the time he wrote these words, James had seen the Messiah of God and the result of people who were prayer warriors.

> Is any one of you in trouble? He should pray. Is anyone happy? Let him sing songs of praise. Is any one of you sick? He should call the elders of the church to pray over him and anoint him with oil in the name of the Lord. And the prayer offered in faith will make the sick person well; the Lord will raise him up. If he has sinned, he will be forgiven. Therefore confess your sins to each other and pray for each other so that you may be healed. The prayer of a righteous man is powerful and effective.
>
> —James 5:13–16

The Effect on History

History hinges on which Ebenezer you choose. When Hophni and Phinehas committed to a lifetime of immorality, they changed history. Their families were destroyed. Thousands of other people died, and countless families were hurt simply because these men, charged with taking care of the things of God, acted foolishly. They compromised themselves, step-by-step, into new areas of disobedience, every day. Just a little compromise today, a bit more tomorrow, and before anyone knew it, these men wearing the title of religious leaders were in a drunken, sexual stupor. Disaster followed.

Disaster will follow any man, any woman, any teenager so foolish as to choose the road of religion. Do the Bible lesson, the sermon, or the Sunday songs of worship have anything to do with your life on Monday? Has the worship of Sunday had any effect on your Fridays and your Saturdays? It would be a foolish, foolish choice to think that there is a difference between the Sunday lessons and the weekday living. To separate the two is to make the choice of Hophni and Phinehas. To choose hypocrisy is to choose the first Ebenezer and to choose to change your future for the worse—much worse.

On the other hand, when Samuel committed to a lifetime of prayer and holiness, he shaped history for the better. "Throughout Samuel's lifetime," the story ends, "the hand of the LORD was against the Philistines. . . . There was peace" (1 Sam. 7:13–14).

Read on in 1 Samuel and you'll see that Samuel anointed and influenced the first two kings of Israel. King Saul—who made mistakes like Hophni and Phinehas—could find no direction in life without Samuel. He even tried to ask Samuel's advice after the old prophet had died. King David also depended on Samuel. Samuel greatly influenced both Saul and David, and the decisions the kings made affected thousands of people.

One day, your impact on history will also be recorded. This is exciting to me. If you choose to live a life of godliness, holiness, and prayer, you will profoundly affect your future.

You can change the future for your children, for your parents, for your grandchildren, by the choices you make today. You can change the future for your community. Praying, fasting, repentant people can tear down Satan's barriers when lawmakers, judges, and community leaders find themselves powerless to do anything at all.

Choosing the path of a relationship instead of the road of religion can have a profound, positive effect on history. Finally, there is one more significant lesson from the life of Samuel and the two Ebenezers.

The Importance of Symbols

Symbols are important ways to keep your relationship with God strong. The word *Ebenezer* means "Stone of Help." Appropriately enough, Samuel set up a great rock right on the road where the Philistines ran for cover. This way, all who passed by would remember that it was God who had helped them, who had won the battle, who had done the work simply because His people had assembled, fasted, confessed their sins, and prayed for help.

No one worshiped the rock, and Samuel never treated it like an idol. It was simply a symbol of a great, miracle-working God.

Samuel himself would pass by that stone countless times. You know what? Samuel needed to see the rock named Ebenezer. There were days of discouragement ahead when he would need to touch it, to rub it, to stop and remember. He needed to remember the thrill of that day when God's people did the right thing and when God's power was in full view of all. God had truly been Samuel's Stone of Help, and it was a wonderful thing to simply go back, touch the rock, and remember.

Do you have a Stone of Ebenezer set up somewhere? Is it a hospital room where you felt the healing power and peace of God? Is it a living room, a bedroom, or a den in a house where you prayed to receive Jesus as your personal Savior? Is it a church baptistery where you took steps of obedience to be baptized as a committed, sold-out follower of Jesus? Is it a retreat center where you first felt the freedom of release and of being filled with the invigorating Spirit of God? Is it a mountain top where you gave your heart to God, saying, "Whatever you want me to do with my life, I'll do it"?

Stones of Ebenezer are powerful reminders. They are things we can touch, things we can see, that represent the things of faith that we can't touch and a God whom we can't see with physical eyes.

You may have read these words only to reach this point, to hear the Spirit of God asking you to establish your own "Rock of Ebenezer." You might be ready to profess Jesus as Savior in an open, public way. You might be ready to be baptized as a sign of your faith. You might be ready to become part of a church family. You might be ready to make a recommitment of your faith, and you might need to mark that recommitment with a stone or a symbol, so that you can come back, years from now, and remember.

It's amazing. Some three thousand years have passed since the history of 1 Samuel took place, but the choice of two Ebenezers is still ours.

Which will you choose?

CHAPTER 3

Beware of the Chicken
of Compromise

Maybe you've heard the story that is making the rounds about the chicken cannon. It seems the Federal Aviation Administration has a device for testing airplane windshields. Try to picture this with me. Workers point a cannon-like instrument at the windshield of an aircraft and shoot a dead chicken at it—at roughly the same speed the plane might meet a real bird in the sky. If the windshield doesn't break, collisions with real birds during flight are not likely to be a problem.

But think about it. A chicken cannon!

The story continues. The British constructed a new locomotive that would pull a train faster than any before it. Since they, too, were concerned about windshield safety, they borrowed the testing device from the FAA, reset it to approximate the maximum speed of the locomotive, loaded in the dead chicken, and fired.

The bird went through the windshield, broke the engineer's chair, and made a dent in the back wall of the engine cab.

As you might imagine, the train testers were quite surprised and troubled with this result. The British asked the FAA to check the cannon to see if everything was done correctly. The review was completed, and as politely as possible the boys from the States made a suggestion. When the test was repeated, said the report, it would be best to use a chicken that wasn't frozen!

How did they miss something so basic? Did they not read the instructions? Did they not see the obvious?

Can I share some words of truth with you? The instructions of God's Word are the only instructions that have ever held truth. You can ignore them if you wish and fire a frozen chicken right through the windshield of your life or of your family's life. You can blow everything to bits if you like, or you can apply the truth of God's Word to your life and survive anything that comes your way.

Sometimes it's not that easy to see the point-blank truth, the easy application of the Bible's instructions. In other times, like the story of Eli's family in 1 Samuel, the truth is easily, clearly seen. This is the story of a family that loaded up a frozen chicken and expected nothing to happen. But the day came when everything was lost. The day came when they faced the full fury of God's wrath.

Allow me, please, to share with you this story of disaster. It is a real picture, so to speak, of a frozen chicken flying through a home, wreaking havoc everywhere, and doing it quickly. The father's name is Eli, a priest and one of the most important leaders of his day. His sons—both priests—are Hophni and Phinehas. This story records the last day of all three men. On their death certificates there might as well have been the notation: "Cause of death: a collision with the chicken of compromise."

More on that later. Right now, read the disaster.

> So the Philistines fought, and the Israelites were defeated and every man fled to his tent. The slaughter was very great; Israel lost thirty thousand foot soldiers. The ark of God was captured, and Eli's two sons, Hophni and Phinehas, died.

That same day a Benjamite ran from the battle line and went to Shiloh, his clothes torn and dust on his head. When he arrived, there was Eli sitting on his chair by the side of the road, watching, because his heart feared for the ark of God. When the man entered the town and told what had happened, the whole town sent up a cry.

Eli heard the outcry and asked, "What is the meaning of this uproar?"

The man hurried over to Eli, who was ninety-eight years old and whose eyes were set so that he could not see. He told Eli, "I have just come from the battle line; I fled from it this very day."

Eli asked, "What happened, my son?"

The man who brought the news replied, "Israel fled before the Philistines, and the army has suffered heavy losses. Also your two sons, Hophni and Phinehas, are dead, and the ark of God has been captured."

When he mentioned the ark of God, Eli fell backward off his chair by the side of the gate. His neck was broken and he died, for he was an old man and heavy. He had led Israel forty years.

His daughter-in-law, the wife of Phinehas, was pregnant and near the time of delivery. When she heard the news that the ark of God had been captured and that her father-in-law and her husband were dead, she went into labor and gave birth, but was overcome by her labor pains. As she was dying, the women attending her said, "Don't despair; you have given birth to a son." But she did not respond or pay any attention.

She named the boy Ichabod, saying, "The glory has departed from Israel"—because of the capture of the ark of God and the deaths of her father-in-law and her husband. She said, "The glory has departed from Israel, for the ark of God has been captured."

—1 Samuel 4:10–22

There's a lot behind the story and several factors that led to the Day of Ichabod. As we consider the story, let's grab some principles that could save our lives from incredible destruction. Here's one idea.

Disrespect Leads to Disaster

According to 1 Samuel 4, on the same day,

- Eli's sons, Hophni and Phinehas, died in battle. They earned a disgraceful place in history and entered eternity known as men who were boldly evil in the very sight of God.
- Eli died of a broken neck when he heard that God had "lost" in battle, for the ark of the covenant had been captured.
- Eli's daughter-in-law died after giving birth to a son she called Ichabod, a name that means "no glory." She, too, thought God had lost.
- An entire nation suffered a great, costly defeat. The ark was gone, more than thirty thousand people were dead, people lost their property and towns, and a nation went into despair.

All of this was the result of blatant disrespect for the things of God. By the way, the ark was fine. In the span of a few weeks, in the span of a few verses of recorded history, it is clear that God had not lost the war. The Philistines kept the ark long enough to realize that this God of Israel was real and that disobeying God and paying no respect to the things of God was a deadly mistake. Ironically, the Philistines then gave more respect to the things of God than the Israelites, and it's the Philistines who were saved. But when the Israelites and Eli's family paid no respect to the things of God, the eventual result was death.

Some three thousand years later, nothing has changed.

If you pay no regard to the things of God today, it will cost you dearly. It will cost you individually, it will cost your family, and it will cost your community. For a generation, we have watched America draw away from God with increasingly open disrespect.

What would you like to consider today? The entertainment industry? Consider that when "Gone with the Wind" premiered, there was national scandal that a four-letter word would be uttered on the silver screen. Today, there is literally nothing that can't be uttered or viewed in the movies, in the videos, in the cable-television broadcasts. What evil is there left to be shown to us? We have moved through compromise, and the day is coming when we will pay dearly. In many ways, that day has already arrived. Children are shooting children in imitation of what they've seen on TV, and a nation's numbness to sexual sin is the result of imitating the "art" we've seen undressed on television and in movies for the past thirty-plus years.

What would you like to consider? What about our addictive nature as a country? We are saturated with alcoholics, drug addicts, gluttons, and sexual perverts. Our country—including huge portions of the Christian community—is loaded with people headed directly for disaster because they have elected to ignore the things of God, the worship of God, the respect of God, and the clear instructions of the Word of God.

What would you like to consider? How about the value of human life? Bathed in all our technology, our record-setting intellect, and our fabulous economy, how is it that we have become the first generation in the history of humanity to disregard the value of life in the human womb? How is it that we are horribly divided, even inside the family of faith, over whether abortion is wrong? Or whether euthanasia is wrong?

What is wrong with us? Are we as morally blind as old Eli? Don't forget that lesson. Before Eli was blind physically, he was blind spiritually and ethically. He turned his eyes away from the wrongs of his family, and the disaster that followed should have been easily foretold. We should never, ever forget to offer forgiveness and healing to those who have made mistakes and wrong choices—especially with those who have chosen abortion in the past—but we must not forget the simple truth that God has set some moral absolutes. To God, all life is precious, and all life must be protected.

What else shall we consider? How about the devaluing of marriage? One generation ago, divorce was incredibly uncommon. Today we congratulate those couples who manage to hang in there for ten or twenty years. Statisticians tell us that today's newlyweds stand, at the most, a fifty-fifty chance of staying married. We've all seen the explosive destruction of divorce. Look around the living room of a divorced home. You'll see children, husbands, wives, parents, and in-laws lying on the battlefield wondering what hit them. They never saw the chicken of compromise that tracked them all down, locking in on their sights until, finally, the Day of Ichabod arrived.

As I write these words, I know that many people won't like what I have to say, and many will disagree. Opinion polls of Americans are showing us shocking things about what we believe. Millions in our country believe there is no real right and wrong and that all truth is relative. But here's what I've found: Opinions, philosophies, and political trends come and go. The only thing that is eternally true is the Word of God, and the Word of God is very, very clear. *Life is precious. Addictions are wrong. Promiscuity and rampant sexual sin is evil.*

When Christians even dabble in these ills, they're dabbling with disaster. They're loading up frozen chickens.

Read the story again and look at dead Eli, dead Hophni, and dead Phinehas. Look at the lifeless body of Phinehas's wife, having just given birth. Like so many others, she was an innocent victim of a man who succumbed to compromise. Just as it was true then, it's true now: Disregard and disrespect for the things of God will lead directly to disaster.

Disaster Begins with Compromise

There is good news. If your prayer today is to avoid the disaster, or if your desperate hope is to correct the mess you might have made of your life already, there *is* hope. But the first part of finding hope is to recognize the pattern of trouble. It's the relief you get when the doctor diagnoses an illness; you may still be sick, but knowing the problem is critically important to curing the problem. So write this diagnosis on your heart: Disaster begins with compromise.

Eli and his sons didn't get to where they were overnight. They didn't wake up one morning and decide to be evil men. It took Eli ninety-eight years to die in the midst of disaster. These men started slowly and worked their way into a mess.

Here's a quick review of how sinful Eli's family had become:

- Eli's sons dove into the deep end of sin. "Eli's sons were wicked men; they had no regard for the LORD" (1 Sam. 2:12).
- They fattened themselves by stealing from the sacrifices (see 1 Sam. 2:13–15).

A bit of explanation is needed. The priests at the tabernacle— that's what Eli's sons were—were to take their living, their food, by taking a three-pronged fork and randomly stabbing some boiled meat from a pot filled with meat that had been sacrificed to God. One stab, one selection, and that was to be enough. If it was small, it was small. If it was chuck roast, it was chuck roast. If it was hamburger, it was hamburger. This was the rule. A priest feeding his family from this selection process wouldn't get fat on such a practice. In fact, he'd have to live a life of great physical discipline. But Eli's sons weren't satisfied with just a little bit of meat. They wanted a lot of meat, and they wanted the finest cuts. They would take the meat before it was cooked and then prepare it to their own taste. To the people of Israel, this must have been a shocking display of self-centeredness. Over the years, through the process of compromise, Hophni and Phinehas became obsessed with physical satisfaction, starting with what they put on their plates. But this wasn't just about poor physical fitness, this was much more about spiritual fitness. They were stealing from God.

- They exhibited their disdain for God before the entire nation, for they had no shame (1 Sam. 2:14).
- They corrupted the servants of the temple (1 Sam. 2:16).
- They had rampant sexual sin. "They slept with the women

who served at the entrance to the Tent of Meeting" (1 Sam. 2:22).

Do you know what's incredible? This is the only time you'll ever see a reference to women serving at the entrance of the tabernacle or the temple. This was something, apparently, that Eli's sons instituted. They liked having a little titillation at the temple. They let their sexual urges go wild, until they were finally having orgies on the church steps. They'd slip around back; they'd go out front; they didn't care. It was rampant sexual sin. They came to a point where they would put it right out there on a big-screen TV and let all the kids watch. They just didn't care.

So far, the sins of Eli's sons had affected the temple servants, some unnamed women, their wives, and the entire nation—a nation watching its spiritual leaders. But guess who else began to compromise? Old, great, wise, faithful Eli.

No words are wasted in Scripture. When we learn from Samuel's record that the ark had been captured, we also learn something else about Eli in his old age.

> When he mentioned the ark of God, Eli fell backward off his chair by the side of the gate. His neck was broken and he died, *for he was an old man and heavy*.
> —1 Samuel 4:18, emphasis added

What does it mean that Eli was heavy? It's more than a physical description. It means that Eli, too, had begun to eat meat stolen from the sacrifices. Can you picture it? Can you smell the temptation? All his life Eli had eaten boiled roast. Now there's a T-bone sizzling on Hophni's grill. Fat Phinehas is laughing, digging into his New York strip, and somebody gets a plate ready for Eli. And one day, probably after years of saying no to such a forbidden practice, Eli succumbs to the temptation and eats the steak. Small sin, yes; no big deal, as big deals go. But by the end of his life, his heart is surrounded by the fat of sin, and he dies a failure. Eli had grown to enjoy the taste of sin.

Hophni and Phinehas weren't men after God's own heart, and their compromise affected their entire family. Some three thousand years later, compromise is still a killer. This time, however, it's your family that's at risk.

Are you a parent? Go slowly.

Parents Are Responsible

God holds parents responsible for a family's compromise and expects parents to take corrective action. Out of loving concern, God sent a nameless prophet, a preacher, to tell Eli to get his family's act together (1 Sam. 2:27–36). The warning came in love. God loved Eli so much that he sent someone to tell him, "Correct your course! You're headed for disaster!" The warning was an effort to get Eli to do *something* to change his family's course.

Like a lot of parents, Eli tried. He told his sons they were wrong. But like a lot of parents, Eli didn't exercise his responsibility to act when his boys wouldn't change their ways. He chose to do nothing (vv. 22–25).

When Eli didn't move beyond words, when he didn't take action, the continued compromises led to more compromises, and eventually, to a day of disaster. On the eve of the promised punishment, God's words came to the old, sin-infested Eli through a boy named Samuel:

> I will carry out against Eli everything I spoke against his family—from beginning to end. For I told him that I would judge his family forever because of the sin *he knew about*; his sons made themselves contemptible, and *he failed to restrain them.*
>
> —1 Samuel 3:12–13, emphasis added

It's unthinkable, but it happened. Old Eli loaded up the frozen chicken, aimed it at his family, and pulled the trigger himself. Everywhere that chicken of compromise went, disaster followed.

If you're a parent, please consider these three principles:

1. Words of warning are not enough.
2. God expects you to take action to correct sin problems.
3. Even if you live for God, your children may not follow the ways of God.

Samuel eventually became a father himself. And what would you know but that his boys followed the ways of Eli's boys. And in time, the day came when Samuel would have to face the same decision that father Eli faced, and that parents the world over still face today. What will you do when children rebel? Read this bit of Scripture and note the difference between Eli and Samuel. Two dads, two different hearts, two different ways of raising a family.

> When Samuel grew old, he appointed his sons as judges for Israel. The name of his firstborn was Joel and the name of his second was Abijah, and they served at Beersheba. But his sons did not walk in his ways. They turned aside after dishonest gain and accepted bribes and perverted justice.
> So all the elders of Israel gathered together and came to Samuel at Ramah. They said to him, "You are old, and your sons do not walk in your ways; now appoint a king to lead us, such as all the other nations have."
> —1 Samuel 8:1–5

Maybe you missed this one. I did, at first. But look closely at the situation. Samuel had sons, and he loved them. Samuel wanted the best for them. He surely used his influence to make them judges, some of the most important men in Israel. However, Samuel's sons, like Eli's sons, did not follow the ways of God. They were sinful. They compromised. They were headed down the same disastrous path. Everything was in danger—their lives, Samuel's life, and the nation's spiritual health.

The people came to Samuel and said, "We want a king." Don't you want the best for your children? Sure you do. You want them to play on the best soccer team, attend the best high school, live in the nicest house possible, be driven in the best vehicle, and have the most respect in your community possible when they become adults. We dream for them. We long for them to have comfort, joy, and success. We sacrifice for them. If the opportunity comes where we can make them "king," so to speak, we do what we can.

Samuel had a great opportunity to anoint one of his sons king. He could have done it. The boys were probably licking their chops, building their egos, getting together a résumé, taking showers, and getting a new suit of clothes. They both hoped their dad would throw his weight around and make the family proud.

But Samuel didn't do it. He had told his sons that their sin was wrong, but his words weren't enough. They hadn't changed as a result of his words. Now, however, Samuel was willing to take action. He withheld something his boys wanted, something that would have changed their lives.

Did you notice the most important detail that's a part of this story? It's hard to see because it's not written down. There is no scalding prophecy against Samuel and his house. There is no disgraceful end to Samuel's life. We never hear from his boys again. Maybe they cleaned up their act. Maybe they sobered up. Maybe they did. Maybe they didn't. But they never had to see a flying, frozen chicken of compromise coming from their father's hand. There was no disaster in Samuel's house, for there was no compromise in Samuel's parenting.

Parents, God expects you to be people not only of words but also of action. Do what it takes to represent your family well before God.

Children Are Also Responsible

Eventually, children are responsible for their own choices. Was it Samuel's fault that his boys turned out wrong? No, it wasn't. Was it Eli's fault that his boys took off on the wild side and got so callused, so *used to* a place called "church," that they would even have illicit sex with people they went to church with? Was it Eli's fault that everyone around them could look and see the obvious truth—that while these boys talked about God, they had not one ounce of respect toward God? No, it wasn't.

Eli and Samuel both took their boys to church, both had shown their sons the things of God, and both had, at least for those early years, been great men of God. Soon enough, Eli's children made their own choices and mistakes, and God took their lives. Samuel's boys made their own choices and mistakes, and Samuel carried out the punishment. In carrying out discipline, Samuel probably saved his boys from the very wrath of God.

Today, the Bible still says these words:

> Do not be deceived: God cannot be mocked. A man reaps what he sows. The one who sows to please his sinful nature, from that nature will reap destruction; the one who sows to please the Spirit, from the Spirit will reap eternal life. Let us not become weary in doing good, for at the proper time we will reap a harvest if we do not give up.
>
> —Galatians 6:7–9

Change Your Future Today

You can change your future with a decision today. The Bible is full of people who were headed down the path of Eli's sons and of Samuel's sons but who heard the warning of God, heeded the words of God, and benefited from the blessings of God as they changed their ways.

There was David, a man who recovered from a deadly mistake late in his life. He became a *greater* man, seeking after God's own heart. There were kings like Rehoboam, Abijah, and Asa—men who saw evil and took action to correct it. There were people like Simon Peter, Zacchaeus, and a nameless thief on the cross. They met Jesus and were transformed.

Throughout history, there must be millions and millions of people who have changed their course and been rescued by the same repentance, the same willingness to actually change evil ways.

Listen again to the testimonies of the Bible. Trusting in Jesus as Savior will change your eternity. Trusting in God's Word as a real, literal guide for living will change your life. God's rules are wonderful, loving, life-giving rules. And God loves you enough to enforce His rules.

As long as you have breath, as long as you have a mind to consider these things, or, as Jesus liked to put it, "eyes to see and ears to hear," you have an opportunity to change your future. You can change your future today, right now. It's as simple as spotting compromise in your lifestyle and eliminating it. Thaw the compromise, and you'll thaw the chicken. You'll survive the battle.

CHAPTER 4

The Heart of a Great Church

Mark Sutton tells the story of a soldier who was wounded in a battle and ordered to the nearest military hospital. When he arrived at the hospital entrance, he saw two doors. One was marked "For Minor Wounds," the other was marked "For Serious Wounds."

He entered the first door and walked down a long hallway. At the end of the hall, he saw two more doors. The first said "For Officers," the other said "For Enlisted Men." The soldier went through the second door.

Again, he found himself walking down a long hallway. Again, he discovered two more doors at the end of that hall. One door said "For Party Members," the other said "For Non-Party Members." The wounded soldier took the second door and found himself back out on the street.

When he got back to his unit, his buddies asked, "How did your trip to the hospital go?"

"To tell you the truth," he said, "the people really didn't help me much, but, man, are they organized!"

Sound like a church you've known? It's the truth! We can be

loaded to the gills with organization but not a lot of help to the walking wounded.

The church has the greatest message ever told, the life-changing reality of what it is to know God! Yet people aren't getting the message. Maybe the church in America is serving up too many bland dishes.

It bothers me that between 3.2 and 5.6 million members of my own denomination—almost one of every three—call themselves church members but hardly ever find time actually to attend church.[1] How I wish those stay-at-home church members could stumble upon Samuel's church.

God Is Able

God is able to make a great church anywhere. It was quite a place, Samuel's church. No walls, no rest rooms, no Christian aerobic and basketball centers. It had no artwork, no plush carpet, no chandeliers. But Samuel's church was full of one thing: the Spirit of the Living God.

> When David had fled and made his escape, he went to Samuel at Ramah and told him all that Saul had done to him. Then he and Samuel went to Naioth and stayed there. Word came to Saul: "David is in Naioth at Ramah"; so he sent men to capture him. But when they saw a group of prophets prophesying, with Samuel standing there as their leader, the Spirit of God came upon Saul's men and they also prophesied. Saul was told about it, and he sent more men, and they prophesied too. Saul sent men a third time, and they also prophesied. Finally, he himself left for Ramah and went to the great cistern at Secu. And he asked, "Where are Samuel and David?"
>
> "Over in Naioth at Ramah," they said.
>
> So Saul went to Naioth at Ramah. But the Spirit of God came even upon him, and he walked along

prophesying until he came to Naioth. He stripped off
his robes and also prophesied in Samuel's presence. He
lay that way all that day and night. This is why people
say, "Is Saul also among the prophets?"

—1 Samuel 19:18–24

What a church! It was full of prophets who were full of the
Spirit of God, and everyone who came into the presence of that
place was changed. *Just walking in,* people were changed. Soldiers
hardened by battle walked in, put down their weapons, and began to prophesy. When Saul, a man overwhelmed with evil, personally came looking for David, he stumbled upon the foyer of
Samuel's church. In moments, the sin-sick king was soon stripped
down to his soul, glorifying God. All across Israel, people heard
about it. "Is Saul also among the prophets?"

Throughout history, God has raised up great churches like that
of Samuel. Just a century ago, New Park Street Baptist Chapel in
London was one of those great churches. Charles Spurgeon was
the pastor there, a position he was given at the ripe old age of
nineteen. The building of New Park Street Chapel was huge. It
could hold fifteen hundred people. Unfortunately, less than two
hundred came on any Sunday.

But something happened at that old church. In a few years, as
many as twenty-three thousand people would hear Spurgeon preach
in a week's time. Newspapers around the world printed his sermons.
When Spurgeon was twenty-eight, the church built the large
Metropolitan Tabernacle to accommodate the large crowds. They
established a school to train pastors and began a book distribution
business. Metropolitan became one of the most famous and
significant religious institutions in nineteenth-century England.
Spurgeon's ministry was particularly known for successfully
attracting people from every walk of life, from the poor of London
to members of Parliament.

But there's a sad part to the story. The church died. When
author and pastor Leith Anderson attended the Metropolitan
Tabernacle in 1972, there were only eighty-seven worshipers

present on that particular Sunday. The speaker lamented over the difficulty in reaching the people in the immediate community of the church. Much had changed in seventy-five years. London had changed, the neighborhood had changed, society had changed, all of the world had changed. But the great church in London had failed to keep up with the changes. Consequently, the church with the greatest message London needed to hear was deathly silent.

But God still works in each generation. Some great churches of our day have changed their methodology—not their message—and reached thousands. Willow Creek in the Chicago area and the Saddleback Community Church in Orange County, California, stand as popular examples of churches that have taken an ancient message of truth into modern cultures and seen God work great miracles.

I'm aware of smaller churches in out-of-the-way places that also catch fire with the Spirit of God and impact their communities. The first church I served saw God bring a wonderful revival in our midst. It was a small place, with thirty-five in Sunday school the day my family arrived. In fact, of those thirty-five, four of them were us! There weren't a lot of people in that part of North Carolina. The nearby railroad tracks had literally been pulled out of the ground. It was ten miles to the nearest large grocery store, and only three families still farmed in what had once been a large farming community.

As we watched in amazement, the church began to grow. In two years, several people had come to Christ and attendance swelled to nearly sixty in Sunday school and more than eighty in worship. It was exciting to be a part of God's work there.

One week stands out in my memory as a time when God visited us. We wanted to do something that hadn't been done in forty years—break one hundred in Sunday school attendance. Since we were only averaging about sixty, it really was going to be a test of faith. To reach our goal on "Miracle Sunday," we arranged to have some home prayer meetings every night for a week. As would be expected, we also prayed for some other things. For one, we prayed for rain. It hadn't rained in weeks, and the crops around us were beginning to suffer greatly. In addition, we prayed for one of our members, Rommie Daniels. "Uncle Rommie" had just been to a large hospital and seen the X rays that showed the suspected spot of lung cancer. He would be rushed to Tennessee, to another large hospital and to a battery of tests. Surgery seemed certain, and his life was in jeopardy.

Rommie picked a good week to have a prayer need. Every night we prayed for rain, for Rommie, and for one hundred in Sunday school.

On "Miracle Sunday" morning, I went to the church to turn on the lights and to spend some time in prayer. It was starting to sprinkle. "Oh, no, Lord, not today!" I prayed. "I know we prayed for rain, but we're trying to have one hundred in Sunday school, and folks just won't come in the rain."

By the time Sunday school was starting, the rain was pouring down. It was raining so hard I had to drive my family to church—and we only lived one hundred yards away. But inside, there were people everywhere. They were wet, they were smiling, and they were ready for Bible study. And when the counting was done, there were one hundred twenty-four of us—an amazing day!

The next day, Uncle Rommie went for his first battery of tests at the hospital in Tennessee. Though doctors held in their hands the original film showing the problem, they could find nothing wrong in Rommie's body! Instead of having surgery, he came home to celebrate his miracle with us.

Know what we had there? A church like Samuel's.

If we take Samuel's church as an example, I think we can find the heart of a great church marked by these four characteristics.

1. *A great church will be led by a leader who is filled with the Spirit of God.* You cannot take your pastor's spiritual health for granted. Every great church has a great number of people praying for its pastor or pastors.
2. *A great church will be filled with other leaders filled with the Spirit of God.* If a church makes the mistake of thinking the

pastor or professional ministers hold the only key to having a great church, it'll fail every time. The body needs leaders in every corner if it is to break away from the crowd and become the place God hopes it will be.

3. *A great church is a place where people feel safe coming for answers.* In this passage, David came looking for confirmation of his call. He was running for his life, and he wanted to see the man who had poured oil on his curly hair years before, claiming that he would be king. "Are you sure, Samuel?" David wanted to ask, just as surely as people are coming to churches all across America with important, critical questions about their lives. Do they feel safe coming into your church? If they want to, can they hide for a while and simply consider the message your church has to deliver?

4. *A great church is where a nation will find its values.* King Saul, the leader of a nation, came out of Samuel's church a changed man. Soon enough, he'd be back to evil ways, but the nation watched that one experience. People knew that, as powerful as their national leader was, a church filled with God's power was much greater. Even Saul couldn't stand in the presence of the living God. Our nation is still watching to see if God is bigger than national leaders, bigger than popular culture.

One Person at a Time

God is able to make a great church anywhere, and He'll make that great church one person at a time. As a matter of fact, that leads me to another major principle: There will come a day when the Spirit of God must fill you and not just your church.

The death of Samuel, as recorded in 1 Samuel 25, must have had a great impact across Israel. "Now Samuel died, and all Israel assembled and mourned for him" (v. 1).

David and Saul both faced a situation that you and I must face. Sooner or later, the church that gave us strength, or the person who was a spiritual mentor for us, will be gone. It can happen in a hundred ways.

- Perhaps you move to another community, and the church in revival is left behind.
- Perhaps your favorite pastor moves away or dies.
- Perhaps your godly parent, the one who was the family's spiritual rock, dies.
- Perhaps the dynamics of your church change, and nothing seems familiar anymore, save the old bricks and the street address.

Sooner or later, you've got to take what was in that great church experience, what was in that great leader, and make it part of your life.

Samuel had grown to be the spiritual giant he was by adhering to some simple principles. Obviously, we can learn from these lessons and apply them to our lives. In fact, taking on these principles is the only way we can avoid the trap of depending completely on another person for our spiritual help. David had to learn it. He survived and grew into a great spiritual leader for his country. Saul couldn't learn it, and he disintegrated into a pitiful pile of rubble at a fortune-teller's table, just a short time before his life came to a tragic end.

Here are the principles I draw from Samuel's heart:

1. Decide as early as possible to love the Lord your God with all your heart, mind, and soul.

Samuel got an early start. He was actually birthed into ministry, held accountable by his mother Hannah's promise, and surrounded by the things of God. The evil of Eli's sons and Eli's compromises had an opposite effect on Samuel. Instead of following the bad examples, he determined that he would serve God first, no matter what.

It's said that the best day to plant a tree was twenty years ago. The next best day to plant a tree is today. Obviously, the best day to have determined to follow God was as long ago as possible. The next best day is today. As you follow this principle, you will enjoy other spiritual giants around you, but you will not be dependent on their walk with God for your own walk with God.

2. Stand firm in your faith, no matter what.

Samuel had to endure wars, the disappearance of the ark of the covenant (the most visible representation of God's presence), and the disappointment of his own sons' lives. Through it all, Samuel remained a great man of God.

If the doctor tells you that the reports from *your* tests have come back with some bad news, will that shake your faith? If the layoffs come into your office unexpectedly, will you still be able to sing praise choruses on the way home? If the romance disappears with an unexpected rejection, will you still love God? If death steals into your home and robs you of the most precious person you've known, will you be able to worship through the tears?

Life is going to throw a lot of trouble at us. Jesus even promised it. "I have told you these things, so that in me you may have peace. In this world you will have trouble. But take heart! I have overcome the world" (John 16:33). The more life throws at you, and the more you stand firm on your faith, the more you will be able to walk as a strong man or woman of God.

3. When given an opportunity, speak the truth in love.

Great Christians aren't the ones who storm into a home with a pointing finger and scream out the sins of a neighbor. If you've ever seen that happen, you know what comes next! People always react in a negative way.

Instead, consider Samuel. And consider him carefully. For if you determine to live for the Lord with all your heart, soul, and mind, if you consistently stand for Christ, sooner or later, God will give you opportunities to speak a word of truth. And people will listen to you. More than likely, they've already listened to everything else, and they've found there's no truth outside of God's Word.

Back to Samuel. When Saul was coming home with a bag full of loot and an attitude full of sin, Samuel met him on the road. Do you remember *why* Samuel was there? He was there to tell Saul that the joyride was over; that God was going to tear the kingdom away from him.

> Then the word of the LORD came to Samuel: "I am grieved that I have made Saul king, because he has turned away from me and has not carried out my instructions."
>
> —1 Samuel 15:10–11

That's right! God sent Samuel to Saul. It was a God-given instruction for Samuel to confront Saul, without any shadow of doubt. On top of that, Samuel loved Saul. The rest of verse 11 tells what Samuel was doing *before* he confronted the sinful king: "Samuel was troubled, and he cried out to the LORD all that night."

By the end of that particular story, Samuel does his best to comfort the somewhat repentant king, but then he has to leave. The words Samuel said to his rebellious king are as real as the ones you may have had to say to a rebellious, teenaged child.

> Then Samuel left for Ramah, but Saul went up to his home in Gibeah of Saul. Until the day Samuel died, he did not go to see Saul again, *though Samuel mourned for him.* And the LORD was grieved that he had made Saul king over Israel.
>
> —1 Samuel 15:34–35, emphasis added

A mature Christian will never take joy in giving a word of correction from the Lord. There will be so much love surrounding the package of correction that it will indeed look like the good medicine that it is. And since none of us—not even Samuel—is perfect, words of correction will be needed throughout life.

4. Be a person of great prayer.

Samuel was a man marked by great prayer. Do you remember the battle with the Philistines at Mizpah? Samuel and the Israelites never forgot it. It's recorded in 1 Samuel 7. It seems the Philistines gathered in great numbers, and the Israelites were terrified. Only God could rescue them, and they begged Samuel to pray as he'd never prayed before. As Samuel prayed, the Lord intervened, and the Israelites won a great battle. Later in his life, Samuel would have such an intimate relationship with the Lord that he would hear critical messages from God about God's country. He would anoint one king and then a second one, having to tell the first king that his reign was over. Samuel was a man of a powerful, time-consuming prayer life.

Never, ever underestimate the power of prayer. Invest so much of your life in prayer that people come to recognize you as a person of prayer.

Could Samuel's Church Be Your Church?

What happens when a godly leader is surrounded by other godly leaders, all following Samuel-like principles? A church develops its own search for God's heart, and that church is blessed beyond measure.

Wesley D. Taylor, of Oregon's Tigard United Methodist Church, tells the story of a severe drought in Santa Rosa, Guatemala, in 1965. People were leaving the city. Businesses were going bankrupt. Crops were perishing. Animals were dying. Special efforts were made to bring water in, but it was scarce everywhere. Catholics were holding special masses. Evangelicals were holding prayer meetings. There was no rain and no water.

Then it happened. In a small Pentecostal meeting, where some believers from the Principe de Pas church had assembled for their regular worship service, the Spirit of the Lord moved in a mighty way. There was a message in tongues, followed a few moments later by an interpretation. It ran like this: "Dig a well in the pastor's backyard. There you will find water."

There was much opposition from other churches as the deacons, elders, and pastor began to dig. They thought these people were fanatics. Maybe they were hallucinating. After all, the pastor's backyard was on a hill. A well should never be dug on a hill, as water always runs low. But the pastor, deacons, and elders all continued to dig. Soon one of the deacons became quite upset. "Why is it in the pastor's backyard?" he asked. "Why couldn't it be in mine?" Another elder thought that maybe the prophecy was biased. One deacon gave up. Another elder left. Even so, a small group pressed on.

Because of the drought, the land was hard, so the digging progressed slowly. On the fourth day, they encountered a big boulder. It was so large they thought they had hit solid rock. The disappointments and frustrations were intensified as another elder left the shoveling team.

But they kept digging around the boulder until finally, after two days, they were able to remove it. Immediately, cold, clear water gushed out! The water poured out of the fresh-water spring, and they began to drink and drink and drink. It was a remarkable sign for the whole town. What the miracle of the well did to the growth of this church carries on to this day. The number of conversions to Christ was staggering; the entire town was influenced by it. Church membership grew from a few dozen to more than nine hundred within that same year.[2] It became a place like Samuel's church—a church with a great heart and a great God.

CHAPTER 5

The Shaping of a Shepherd's Heart

What a great story it was. A tourist approached an old codger in a little village and asked, "Hey mister—any great people born in this town?" "Naw," drawled the old man, "never had anything but babies born here."

It's the story of Abraham Lincoln growing up in a log cabin far removed from any town. Who would have known that the gangly child in the woods would one day, after many failures, become one of the great leaders in human history?

It's the story of baseball legend Jackie Robinson. Did you know he was born just outside Cairo, Georgia? Most of the folks who live within one hundred miles of the place probably don't know that bit of sports trivia. Take the drive there today, and you'll see that all that remains of baby Jackie's birthplace is the kudzu-covered brick chimney that once anchored a poverty-stricken black woman's home. She was a single mother frantically looking for a way to survive, and soon she'd leave Georgia looking for hope.[1] She took her infant son with her, a boy behind the eight ball of life. Who would have known how this child would quietly change race relations in America?

It's the story of Helen Keller, born into the loneliness of blind and silent obscurity. Who would have known that her struggle to read, to write, to communicate would teach us all about the value of every life?

God knew, just as God knows what kind of royal potential is in your life.

Beginning with a Childlike Heart

Don't imagine for a moment that David was a king right from the beginning. For most of his childhood, the boy must have wondered if anyone knew he was alive. It's one thing to take a vacation in the woods, to take a drive through the mountains, or to camp out underneath the stars and take a break from lifestyles that move at the speed of microchip calculations. It's a different matter to be exiled to the pastures, while everyone else in the world is in town making life happen. He was a prisoner in open spaces.

Out there in the fields, David could have thought about how badly things were going. It wasn't a secret that he wasn't number one in his family's eyes. He had been pushed so far out to pasture, so far in the background, that he wasn't even called when the prophet Samuel came to lunch. He had a dull, menial kind of job. For centuries, people have counted sheep to fall asleep. David had to count them for his job! He spent a lot of time by himself. He wasn't an only child, he was a *lonely* child.

David did have some strengths as a child, but no more than most children. The Bible speaks of him having a ruddy, fine appearance, with handsome features. He was healthy. He'd been outdoors most of his life. He had musical gifts, and he wasn't ashamed to use them. It didn't matter that the gifts were musical and not mathematical or not in the field of, say, science. He simply took what he had an ability to do, and he used it. He had a harp and plenty of time to play it. And talk about strengths, David was obedient to his parents. They needed him to do a good job in the pastures, and he did it. Watching sheep is tedious work. More so than any other animal, sheep need a lot of care. David did a good job in his work.

Even after the young teenager was anointed king—a rather lofty incident—and after David had actually spent time in the king's palace with the king himself, David remained obedient to his father. David had been where his dad had never been, but he remained humble. "Son," said Jesse, "I need you to run some bread to your brothers. I want to know how they're doing." "Sure, Dad," said David, and he was off.

Good things were happening to this boy. He didn't know it then, but yes, he would become a great man of history. Did you know that David's name appears nearly nine hundred times in the Bible? David is mentioned more times than any other person except Jesus Himself. But those days of glory were a long, long way off. Out there in sheepish surroundings, a boy's heart was being shaped and molded.

If there is any interest in your heart in finding the heart of God, take a long look at the boy when the Bible introduces us to him. He's out in the fields when Samuel the prophet comes to Jesse's town, told by the Spirit of God that a son of Jesse will be Israel's next king. The first clue to finding what's in David's heart is in finding what's not in his oldest brother's heart.

As the family meets Samuel, Eliab, the oldest son of Jesse, throws his head back and sticks his chest out. He has biceps that bulge and a steely look in his eyes. "The search is over," thought the prophet. "This Eliab is made to be a king."

God had different plans and a different king in mind. Actually, God had a different *heart* in mind, a heart that had already been made tender by His heart. Eliab wasn't the man in God's mind.

> When they arrived, Samuel saw Eliab and thought, "Surely the Lord's anointed stands here before the Lord."

But the LORD said to Samuel, "Do not consider his
appearance or his height, for I have rejected him. The
LORD does not look at the things man looks at. Man
looks at the outward appearance, but the LORD looks at
the heart."

Then Jesse called Abinadab and had him pass in front
of Samuel. But Samuel said, "The LORD has not chosen
this one either." Jesse then had Shammah pass by, but
Samuel said, "Nor has the LORD chosen this one." Jesse
had seven of his sons pass before Samuel, but Samuel
said to him, "The LORD has not chosen these." So he
asked Jesse, "Are these all the sons you have?"

"There is still the youngest," Jesse answered, "but he
is tending the sheep."

Samuel said, "Send for him; we will not sit down until he arrives."

So he sent and had him brought in. He was ruddy,
with a fine appearance and handsome features.

Then the LORD said, "Rise and anoint him; he is the
one."

So Samuel took the horn of oil and anointed him in
the presence of his brothers, and from that day on the
Spirit of the LORD came upon David in power. Samuel
then went to Ramah.

                                        —1 Samuel 16:6–13

Looking for a King's Heart

Want to see Eliab's heart? It's important, for it was this young
man's heart that God had seen and rejected for His next king.
Flip over a page in your Bible to 1 Samuel 17:26. David has come
to the battlefield with provisions for his brothers, found a giant
with a filthy mouth, and asked some important questions. "What
will be done for the man who kills this Philistine and removes this
disgrace from Israel? Who is this uncircumcised Philistine that he
should defy the armies of the living God?"

Eliab was there, a trained soldier, a great physical specimen, a man capable of battle. His heart and his lack of faith, however, had kept him from the miracle of watching God defeat the giant. Eliab and the others on the hillside had decided it was easier to listen to Goliath's curses than to take the walk of faith that might lead to death. They weren't ready to die for the Lord they professed.

The defeat of his heart burned in Eliab's soul. When his baby brother asked painful questions, Eliab couldn't take it. The kid had come to embarrass them all, nothing more.

> When Eliab, David's oldest brother, heard him speaking with the men, he burned with anger at him and asked, "Why have you come down here? And with whom did you leave those few sheep in the desert? I know how conceited you are and how wicked your heart is; you came down only to watch the battle."
>
> "Now what have I done?" said David. "Can't I even speak?"
>
> —1 Samuel 17:28–29

Did you hear the rage? Do you feel the frustration of faithlessness in Eliab's voice? That's the heart that God had seen weeks before when Samuel was ready to make the older brother a king. It was the heart—it was Eliab's faith—that wasn't strong enough. God saw the inside, and God knew the truth: There was no king inside Eliab.

But out in the pasture, under the stars, under the blazing sun, a boy's heart was finding faith in small but important ways.

Finding Faith in Life's Experiences

First, there was the bear. Remember the story? David told it while trying to convince Saul that he could, indeed, tackle a large Philistine (1 Sam. 17:34–37). I wonder what it was like, going one-on-one with a bear. There was another incident, too, when the

rustling in the weeds turned out to be a lion. What a confronta-
tion—the king of the jungle meeting one of the King's kids! David
got between the lion and the sheep, used his brain, checked his
heart, and then used his weapon, a shepherd's rod. The rod was a
heavy, clublike instrument used in threatening times like this. The
lion died, just as the bear had died, and David had another trophy kill.

I think David learned a lot more from those encounters than
how to employ the pointers from the latest Hebrew issue of *Field
and Stream*. David was under no illusion that he had Samson-like
strength to overpower full-grown predators. No, it was God who
had given him victory, and the teenager was quick to admit it
(v. 37). It had taken courage, it had taken skill, but God had pro-
vided both. The encounters made the kid mighty confident of
the battles that would lie ahead, because it was in the sheep fields
that David had learned of the power of God. When David was
much older, he wrote the words of Psalm 71:5: "For you have
been my hope, O Sovereign LORD, my confidence since my youth."

Maybe I'm writing to a child today, one who wonders how in
this big old world any good is going to come out of her life. She
remains hidden in a windowless classroom, trying to learn some
school-room equations she's convinced she'll never use again. Who,
besides a handful of people, even knows she's alive? Or maybe it's
a young man, stuck on the bench of his school's basketball team,
knowing that time is running out on his chance to stand out from
the crowd. Maybe it's a young adult trapped in an unappreciated,
unknown job, grinding through the forty-hour work week, listening to Top 40 songs on the company radio, trying to forget that
the dream once pursued hasn't become reality. How will life ever
have any meaning, any joy, any purpose? Maybe it's another story;
maybe it's your story.

Look at David, a man after God's own heart, when he was only
a boy finding God's heart. Out there in the lonely fields of
Bethlehem, he instinctively looked for what God was doing. As
the afternoons drifted by, David had some choices of attitude. He
could sit and sulk, or he could become the very best shepherd his

village had ever known. He could cry himself to sleep at night at his forgotten state, or he could discover a God-given song-writing ability that would create the greatest songs the world has ever known. When the opportunity came to trust God, he could run for help or fight bears and lions with the Help he had. Over and over, David had choices of attitude. Every choice—whether for good or bad—was shaping his heart.

And what do you know? It looks as if God gave David a few bear-and-lion tests to cut his teeth on so that in a few years, he'd show an entire nation what the Lord could do with real giants.

Here are a couple of things that jump out at us from the Bible's description of David's early days.

1. God wants to use the experiences of your life to prepare you for your life's purpose.

Not everyone takes advantage of those early experiences. Eliab probably spent a lot of time in the same pastures as his baby brother. David simply learned what was meant to be learned there. Has it occurred to you that God might have you right where He wants you? Or that you grew up exactly where God placed you? Romans 8:28 reminds us that He is able to work good in every situation for those who are called by Him, according to His purposes.

2. God is in control of timing.

David was anointed king as a youth, but he was thirty before he claimed his throne. It would be another seven and a half years before he would secure his rule over all Israel. In between childhood and kingship, there must have been a lot of wondering about God's timing. Some of the great songs David wrote dealt with exactly that issue. Psalm 13 begins with the haunting words: "How long, O LORD? Will you forget me forever? How long will you hide your face from me?" (v. 1).

David would find, just as you and I find, that God is in control of timing. David needed every quiet moment in the pastures of seclusion in order to prepare for the noise of the future. His heart needed molding. If God's timing seems delayed today, relax and know that, in reality, God is in control.

3. You're responsible for the search for God's heart.

Everyone has opportunities to benefit from life's experiences. Everyone has God's timing laid out in the blueprint of heaven. But few find the faith it takes to search for God's heart.

When David faced Goliath, all Israel would find that God didn't need someone famous to work a miracle. As a matter of fact, God didn't need a trained soldier or a seasoned adult to do the job. God only needed someone who shared His heart. Out in the pastureland, watching sheep, talking to God, trusting God, David had found God's heart. He found it early. That heart that had searched for God's heart would turn out to be David's greatest strength, all the way through his long and eventful life.

Did David write the words to his best-known song, Psalm 23, early in his life? I suspect, on a day when things were going very well, that David reflected all the way back to his childhood, to those long days on the grassy plateau near his home, and he became like one of his sheep—a very contented sheep.

> The LORD is my shepherd, I shall not be in want.
>> He makes me lie down in green pastures,
> he leads me beside quiet waters,
>> he restores my soul.
> He guides me in paths of righteousness
>> for his name's sake.
> Even though I walk
>> through the valley of the shadow of death,
> I will fear no evil,
>> for you are with me;
> your rod and your staff,
>> they comfort me.

You prepare a table before me
    in the presence of my enemies.
You anoint my head with oil;
    my cup overflows.
Surely goodness and love will follow me
    all the days of my life,
and I will dwell in the house of the LORD
    forever.

                        —Psalm 23

When a boy's heart is turned toward God, it stays there. There is no other place to go. There's just no other security like the security of knowing the Shepherd.

Have you found that security? Perhaps your prayer today should be for a bit of time in the pasture, learning from the sheep how to trust the Shepherd. It's never too late to become a child again, trusting God's plan of salvation with a childlike faith.

Perhaps it's God's timetable that you need to trust. Loneliness, a few bears and lions, even some cutting words from an older brother, proved to make David's heart a heart that was after God's heart. Couldn't the circumstances of your life today be preparation for tomorrow's battles?

Another Shepherd from Bethlehem

From the line of David came a Messiah, and his name was Jesus Christ. Born in David's birthplace, Jesus of Bethlehem was Jesus the Savior. Perhaps Jesus thought of David the shepherd, the one with the trusting heart, when He spoke these words:

Therefore Jesus said again, "I tell you the truth, I am the gate for the sheep. All who ever came before me were thieves and robbers, but the sheep did not listen to them. I am the gate; whoever enters through me will be saved. He will come in and go out, and find pasture. The thief comes only to steal and kill and destroy; I

have come that they may have life, and have it to the
full. . . .

"I am the good shepherd; I know my sheep and my
sheep know me—just as the Father knows me and I know
the Father—and I lay down my life for the sheep."

—John 10:7–10, 14–15

You don't have to go to Bethlehem to find the pastoral peace
David found. You can find it right where you are. If you've never
done so, you can find that peace today. Right now, trust Jesus
Christ as your Shepherd, your Savior, and turn your life over to
Him. Find a body of Christian believers and grow in the knowledge of what it is to take on the name of Christ. You will soon
find how wonderful the search for God's heart can be.

CHAPTER 6

Decisions of the Heart

One of the few places more confining than the front seat of a compact car is the front seat of a heart that must make a crucial decision. Life-changing decisions tend to make us uncomfortable, even when we know what we must do.

We had dated for more than two years, and there had been little doubt along the way that our love relationship would last a lifetime. But was the time really right to hand her the box hidden between the bucket seats? She was inches away from a question that would change her life. Through the entire evening, I was the only person in the car who knew about the golden ring with the small diamond, the ring that could change everything.

When we drove into her parents' driveway, it was a now-or-never moment. We made small talk for a moment, but it was clearly time to pop the question or put it off forever.

Don't we all eventually come to the driveway of decision?

Life Demands Decisions

Do you remember Jonathan and his day of decision? Jonathan was the son of Saul and the greatest friend David ever had.

It seems a battle had come to a standstill. The enemy was on one side of the valley, the army of God on the other side. In Jonathan's case, the enemy was a Philistine army. In your case, the enemy could be a financial problem, a sudden bout with illness, or a decision that has kept you restless for weeks.

Jonathan was looking a decision squarely in the face when things weren't going well. The enemy was huge. "The Philistines assembled to fight Israel, with three thousand chariots, six thousand charioteers, and soldiers as numerous as the sand on the seashore" (1 Sam. 13:5).

It was a distressing time, and no one seemed ready to step up to the plate and hit a winning home run. It looked for all the world as if anyone who tried, in this situation, was going to strike out and be immortalized as the man who lost the World Series. Who wanted that kind of reputation?

> When the men of Israel *saw that their situation was critical* and that their army was hard pressed, they hid in caves and thickets, among the rocks, and in pits and cisterns. Some Hebrews even crossed the Jordan to the land of Gad and Gilead.
>
> Saul remained at Gilgal, and all the troops with him were *quaking with fear.*
>
> —1 Samuel 13:6–7, emphasis added

In all, some twenty-four hundred soldiers headed for home. Only six hundred were hiding in the bushes, trying to look like a brave army. They weren't faking it very well. In fact, the Bible says they were quaking!

Who could blame the shaken or the defectors? The Philistines were well armed and well stocked. There were thousands of them, and all the smart money had already buried the Israelite army. Only two men wearing Israel's colors even had a sword or spear.

One of the weapon-holders was the king, King Saul.

The other was his son, Jonathan.

Now hang on. The lesson of the valley that follows may become very important to you. Apparently several days passed. There was a stalemate between the half-hiding Israelites and the well-oiled Philistines. Obviously, when the Philistines headed into the valley, there would be a brief battle, an immense slaughter, and only a few of Jonathan's kinsmen would survive.

The person who should have made the decision, of course, was the king. But for most of his life, Saul had trouble making right decisions. Saul had trouble with his faith, with his courage, with his heart. He had already been in some tight spots, already taken too many called third strikes, already bobbled too many ninth-inning ground balls for game-losing errors. Saul had a "don't-lose" mentality, and he had lost a hundred games.

Jonathan, however, was ready to make a decision. Hadn't God promised to fight for Israel? Hadn't the great fighters of Israel—Joshua, Gideon, Samson—been forced into the valley of winner-take-all? Hadn't the great men of God battled insurmountable odds and won? This was his valley, this was his day of decision. This was the day when Jonathan would turn his heart toward God.

Without telling his father, Jonathan offered his armor-bearer a chance to die. The two of them would slip down the safe side of the mountain, cross the open valley, climb quickly to enemy territory, and then defeat thousands of well-armed Philistines.

To put it mildly, it was an absurd plan.

But big hearts can come in small packages, and the unnamed armor-bearer agreed. I believe it was at the edge of the valley that they had one final conversation, these two young desperados. For a few final seconds, they were still hidden. The plan was still their secret. No one knew they were there. But once they set foot in the valley, their plan would be exposed for all to see. Thousands of enemies would tense for the attack, thirsting for some bloody action. Once they were out in the open, hundreds of the home fans would see that the battle had been pressed, that these two boy-men had decided to die.

The glimpse of Jonathan's heart came at the edge of that valley, when there was still time to turn back.

> Jonathan said to his young armor-bearer, "Come, let's go over to the outpost of those uncircumcised fellows. Perhaps the LORD will act in our behalf. Nothing can hinder the LORD from saving, whether by many or by few."
> "Do all that you have in mind," his armor-bearer said. "Go ahead; I am with you heart and soul."
> —1 Samuel 14:6–7

The story has a great ending. The Philistines taunted the two-man enemy attack, but the two young Israelites climbed the cliff and defeated twenty Philistines. There was blood dripping off Jonathan's sword, and there was victory in the way he squared his shoulders, looking for the next pocket of twenty enemies. Within moments a few Philistines started running for cover, and then there were hundreds running. Panic overtook the army, and the battle turned into a footrace. The six hundred Israelites woke from their troubled slumber, chased the enemy, secured the land, and stocked their armories with Philistine weapons.

It's Still Up to You!

Now here's the unusual part. Some folks can watch a miracle take place in valleys like Jonathan's, and still not believe the reality of God.

How could Saul not believe in God's power, when his son had led a God-sized victory? How can people today hear stories of changed lives, of miracles given, of faith rewarded, and not take a chance on God?

Saul is only one Bible chapter away from losing his job as God's king. He'll hold the title, the crown, and the throne room for a short time more, but God sends a message through Samuel, the prophet, that a kingly replacement is already on the way. It's a boy, says the prophet, who has searched for God's heart.

Later on, David will have to face Goliath in a valley much like Jonathan's. Again, Saul will be hiding behind the rocks of the home team, hesitating on the day of decision. It will be up to him, and he won't be able to make the decision of faith. All of his life, Saul could *never* choose faith. The only decisions he seemed to make were decisions not to decide.

Centuries later, the disciples would hear the instructions of Jesus and wonder if this Messiah hopeful had lost his mind. Jesus was sending them out, two-by-two, without so much as a credit card—no money, no extra clothes, no food. They would be walking by faith into a valley of trust, a valley of watching God provide for every need in the nick of God's timing. In the face of a tough decision, those followers of Christ walked toward the future in faith.

Later on, a missionary named Paul would head into valleys of his own. He would be beaten, imprisoned, and nearly killed. But faced with the valley of decision, Paul reached a point of always—*always*–heading into the valley. Only there could he find the miracles of God. As he crossed the valley of faith, Paul found that earthquakes could open prison doors, execution attempts would fail, riots would quiet, and provisions would be given when he was on the verge of starvation.

Valleys like Jonathan's are ever before us. May I share some other lessons from Jonathan's heart?

1. You can't use your family's faults as an excuse to fail.

You talk about a dysfunctional and rough home life—Jonathan grew up with King Saul as a father. How Jonathan learned to have a heart of faith is beyond me. The boy rarely heard his dad speak of God at all, much less speak *to* God. If you want to determine Jonathan's success in God's eyes by what he grew up watching, the kid doesn't stand a chance.

I have met dozens of godly men and women who had to over-come a bad influence at home. You've met them, too. Maybe you grew up in a dysfunctional home. Sometimes the blame can be laid on alcohol, sometimes on pornography, sometimes on men-tal illness, sometimes on blatant evil.

When it came to a test of faith, God didn't allow Jonathan to use his father's faithlessness as an excuse. You can't use that ex-cuse, either. As a matter of fact, like Jonathan, you can win great battles for the Lord no matter what your other family members have done or are doing.

2. Stay in the wake of Christ, and you'll win the battles.

Look at the armor-bearer for a moment. What a great picture!

> Jonathan climbed up, using his hands and feet, with his armor-bearer *right behind him.* The Philistines fell be-fore Jonathan, and his armor-bearer *followed and killed behind him.* In that first attack Jonathan and his armor-bearer killed some twenty men in an area of about half an acre.
>
> —1 Samuel 14:13–14, emphasis added

Today, you'll win battles for the Lord only if you stay behind your champion, Jesus Christ. When I signed up to be a Christian, I had no idea of the spiritual battles that would follow. Most people I see giving their hearts to Christ are not aware that there is a spiritual war raging all around us. But soon enough, they'll feel the temptation, they'll see the attacks, they'll feel the heat of the battle.

Are you in the battle today? Stay with Christ, turning to neither the right nor the left. Listen to the words of the Bible and follow them literally.

Here's a different illustration of the same principle. I remem-ber learning how to water-ski many, many years ago. What a struggle it was! After nearly drowning, I was suddenly up on the water. That power boat pulled me all around the lake. What an exhilarating feeling! As hard as it was getting up on the water, the smooth wake directly behind the boat quickly made things easier in my new pastime. In fact, skiing in the wake was so smooth, it soon became boring. After a few minutes of easy skiing, I decided to leave the wake and cross over to the choppy waters outside the wake. I had seen the experienced skiers throwing up great "rooster tails" of spray as they skied back and forth across the wake, and I wanted to do that.

If you've ever seen a skier cartwheel head over heels with skis headed in opposite directions, if you've ever seen a boy flying through the air toward an unquestioned liquid disaster, then you can imagine what I looked like the first time I left the wake. It was a bad, bad idea for me to leave the wake.

Leaving the wake of Christ as a Christian is no simple fall on the water. When teenagers leave the wake of Christ sexually, many of them wind up with an unexpected pregnancy, the horrendous memory of an abortion, or even a deadly disease. When adults leave the wake of Christ, they often lose their jobs, their good names, even their families. When pastors leave the wake, they often lose their ministries, their families, and their joy.

Take the lesson of Jonathan's valley of decision: Stay behind your champion and share in His victory.

3. Bear the armor for your own protection.

Jonathan and his armor-bearer literally wore protection for the battle. They put it all on. They checked the buckles, they tested their shoulder pads, tugged on their helmets, and they made sure they could move about as easily as possible.

If you're a Christian, you've been told to wear armor, too.

> Finally, be strong in the Lord and in his mighty power. Put on the full armor of God so that you can take your stand against the devil's schemes. For our struggle is not against flesh and blood, but against the rulers,

against the authorities, against the powers of this dark world and against the spiritual forces of evil in the heavenly realms. Therefore put on the full armor of God, so that when the day of evil comes, you may be able to stand your ground, and after you have done everything, to stand. Stand firm then, with the belt of truth buckled around your waist, with the breastplate of righteousness in place, and with your feet fitted with the readiness that comes from the gospel of peace. In addition to all this, take up the shield of faith, with which you can extinguish all the flaming arrows of the evil one. Take the helmet of salvation and the sword of the Spirit, which is the word of God. And pray in the Spirit on all occasions with all kinds of prayers and requests. With this in mind, be alert and always keep on praying for all the saints.

—Ephesians 6:10–18

Whose armor are we to wear? *God's* armor. Wear it all! Stay in the wake of Christ! And no excuses. Today might be your day of decision!

About That Ring . . .

Mind you, the valley may look more like the job application in your hand, the challenge you hear in a sermon, or the driveway of your future in-laws.

"I've got something for you," said the boy with the trembling voice, "but first, you've got to answer a question."

She waited on the question of the night, not aware that it was really a question of a lifetime. Her answer, her decision, would change everything.

"Do you want to get married?"

And miracle of miracles, the Philistines ran, the battle was won—and she said yes.

Whether she says yes or whether she says no, whether the job offer comes through or the new business starts successfully, whether the challenge heard is accepted or put aside, you and I will continue to make critical decisions at the edge of decision-making valleys.

A man or woman, a teenager, a boy or girl must decide whether or not to cross the valley with Jonathan or hide in the bushes with Saul. It's there, at the edge of the valley, that you will find your answer if you have a heart searching for God's own heart.

CHAPTER 7

The Heart of a Great Leader

It was several centuries ago when a French peasant by the name of Joan of Arc was called to save her country from its enemies. She had a sacred sword, a consecrated banner, and an undying belief in her mission. The French, under her leadership, swept to amazing victories over strong enemies.

According to the story, in the midst of one battle, someone needed to lead a charge. Joan of Arc was ready. "I will lead the men over the wall," she said to one of her generals. The general said, "Not a man will follow you."

Joan of Arc replied, "I won't be looking back to see if they're following me."

I love it! Great leadership comes from great hearts. For Joan of Arc, radical leadership led to execution at age nineteen. As she was about to be burned at the stake, this nineteen-year-old was given a chance to recant; she was given a chance for liberty and freedom. But she chose the fire, and going to her death she made this statement: "Every man gives his life for what he believes, and every woman gives her life for what she believes. Sometimes people believe in little or nothing, and yet they give their lives to that little or nothing. One life is all we have; we live it, and it's gone. But to live without belief is more terrible than dying, even more terrible than dying young."

Centuries before Joan of Arc was ready to die for a godly cause, God needed a leader on the hillsides of southwest Israel. Thankfully, God had been preparing the heart of a young man who was earnestly seeking God's heart, a young man ready to tackle any giant in God's way.

Waiting on Godly Leaders

The success of God's army depends on godly leaders, but the story told in 1 Samuel 17 begins with a huge problem. God's army is gathered together, but no one will step into the leadership position that King Saul has vacated. Saul is on location, mind you, but he's not leading. This great story starts with this negative. Saul wouldn't be the godly leader that the Lord needed.

Goliath saw it. "Are you not the servants of Saul?" asked the giant in giant-sized derision (1 Sam. 17:8). He was not impressed with what he saw, and there certainly was no fear of the Lord on either side of the battle line.

David saw it. "Who is this uncircumcised Philistine that he should defy the armies of the living God?" (v. 26). Why in the world isn't somebody on God's side doing something about this mess?

But this army was helpless. The armies were on opposite mountains, with a valley of faith between them, and the enemy of God's people was making a mockery of the power of God. When God's people wouldn't step out in faith, they were saying more about what they believed about God than about what they believed about themselves. Saul and his army didn't have a big enough God!

Remember, Saul had been working on vacating his leadership responsibilities for a long, long time. Study his life in 1 Samuel. You find overwhelming evidence that Saul served himself and not God. Saul neglected, for years, the things of God.

Consider these things. The record of Saul's life shows almost no personal prayer. There is almost no public leadership in worship. At one point, folks were stunned that he had stopped to build an altar. The words of 1 Samuel 14:35 tell us: "Then Saul built an altar to the LORD; it was the first time he had done this." Imagine the Bible's historian being so surprised at this act of worship that he would devote a special sentence to it. He's telling us that it was the first time the king—the king of *God's* nation—had done such a thing. Apparently, Saul wasn't much at worship, for the king is never recorded singing so much as the verse of a single song.

On the other hand, David's worship and worship songs came straight from the heart, and they came often. The Bible devotes a huge section of its pages to David's songs. David was a man not afraid to worship with reckless abandon.

Saul, however, was no David. After years and years of neglecting his faith in safe spots, Saul had no faith in a dangerous situation. This is not the first time Saul had been afraid of God's Philistine enemies, but Goliath represented how far from faith Saul had fallen.

The end result is tragic. "God's army" cowered before a defeatable enemy. How easy would it be to defeat this enemy? Incredibly easy. Why, a boy with a slingshot would eventually carry the day.

The cut-to-the-core words of 1 Samuel 17:11 tell us: "On hearing the Philistine's words, Saul and all the Israelites were dismayed and terrified."

Who bore most of the blame? Saul, the leader.

Can you see the obvious lesson for us? Satan is a defeated enemy. He has no right to come against us. Yet many of God's people, even entire churches, are dismayed and terrified at the idea of tackling thorny issues in their midst. The short answer to the problem? God's people are waiting on godly leaders to step forward in faith. As a matter of fact, God Himself is waiting on godly leaders!

Making a Difference

One God-trusting leader can make a difference for all of God's people. Think of some examples. One woman decides to tackle drunk-drivers in her community and ignites a national movement that wakes a slumbering nation out of its deadly, drunken sleep. One person decides to share his faith and single-handedly leads a period of revival for an entire church. One pastor decides to stand up to evil in his community and single-handedly causes laws to be changed and immoral businesses to close.

In 1 Samuel, that one person who made a difference was David, a teenager after God's own heart. David walked into the Israelite camp, asked a few questions, and soon enough found himself leading a military charge for his country. He was one person, doing one thing, for the One who had already proved Himself faithful.

Harry Truman, a president characterized by his uncompromising leadership, said these words: "How far would Moses have gone if he had taken a poll in Egypt? What would Jesus Christ have preached if he had taken a poll in the land of Israel? What would have happened to the Reformation if Martin Luther had taken a poll? It isn't polls or public opinion of the moment that counts. It is right and wrong and leadership."

One leader can change history, armed with nothing more than a slingshot, five stones, and a heart that belongs to God.

Expecting Criticism

In the heady success of godly leadership, please be cautioned. The road is rarely smooth or full of pleasant traveling. If you dare to lead, expect criticism!

Abraham Lincoln, perhaps the most beloved president of the United States, was also the most criticized president. In 1863, the *Chicago Times* evaluated a speech Lincoln made. The writer was scathing in the criticism. "The cheek of every American," said the article, "must tingle with shame as he reads the silly, flat, and dish-watery utterances of a man who has been pointed out to intelligent foreigners as President of the United States." Know what speech the newspaper panned? A rather short one that came to be known as the "Gettysburg Address."

So brace yourself. If you play baseball, you'll take the risk of striking out on a regular basis and bobbling a few ground balls that should have been easy plays. If you play a violin, you take the risk of missing a note during your solo. If you lead people, non-leaders will take their shots at you, even if God does have His hand upon you! And that's a guarantee.

> David asked the men standing near him, "What will be done for the man who kills this Philistine and removes this disgrace from Israel? Who is this uncircumcised Philistine that he should defy the armies of the living God?"
>
> They repeated to him what they had been saying and told him, "This is what will be done for the man who kills him."
>
> When Eliab, David's oldest brother, heard him speaking with the men, he burned with anger at him and asked, "Why have you come down here? And with whom did you leave those few sheep in the desert? I know how conceited you are and how wicked your heart is; you came down only to watch the battle."
>
> "Now what have I done?" said David. "Can't I even speak?" He then turned away to someone else and brought up the same matter, and the men answered him as before. What David said was overheard and reported to Saul, and Saul sent for him.
>
> —1 Samuel 17:26–31

Just as David got ready to lead he took some bitter, critical, unfair shots from his own brother. The giant in the valley, the enemy, hadn't said an unkind word to him. But from his family came some cruel, biting words. Have you felt words like that? Few people haven't. But if you want to be that godly leader who will motivate God's people, you might as well get ready for criticism.

One of the things I love about this story is the way David dealt with the criticism. In fact, the Bible gives us, right here, some great lessons for leadership.

1. *Don't argue with your critic.* Had David set about proving to his older brother that he wasn't deserving of the words "conceited" and "wicked," he'd have never gotten around to Goliath, the real enemy. Did it sting David to be criticized? You bet. "Now what have I done?" he protested. "Can't I even speak?" Though David clearly disagreed with his critic, he said nothing more, refusing to enter an extended argument.

2. *Remain focused on the legitimate problem.* Goliath was the problem, not discouraged Eliab. Immediately, David turned to other soldiers and asked for details.

3. *Let God prove your critic wrong.* In time, God did a great thing for David and the Israelites. No one doubted that God was involved in this battle. A boy, a slingshot, a stone? No way was the enemy army afraid of this child. No, this army was now afraid of this child's God. David made a wonderful habit of letting God take care of his problem people. In time, God would bring down every enemy David had.

4. *Don't hold a grudge against your critic.* A few pages over, in 1 Samuel 22, we find that David gathers a small army together, about four hundred men strong. Know who signed up first? "When his brothers and his father's household heard about it, they went down to him there. . . . And he became their leader" (vv. 1–2). Eliab certainly had to apologize for his words, and David must have forgiven him. You can almost hear David: "Look, Eliab, I understand. It was war, and things hadn't been going well. It was understandable to be a bit testy, to speak too quickly, too harshly." No grudge there. The past was where it should have been—in the *past.* No need to waste time. After all, Goliath had brothers, and Saul was a major problem. You, too, if you're going to be a leader, have too many real enemies to waste time on holding grudges against every critic.

Defining Leadership by Action

Leadership is determined by the heart and defined by action. David's heart had been prepared in the pastures of Bethlehem, and there would be one more heart-check at a creek bank.

After David was hauled in front of King Saul, he had a few moments of modeling some man-sized armor. When he finally took off the much-too-large armor, David finally had permission from the king to die. "Go," said Saul, "and the LORD be with you" (17:37). As far as Saul could see, the kid had no armor, no help, and no hope.

Have you ever pictured the scene that followed? "Then he took his staff in his hand," reads 17:40, "chose five smooth stones from the stream, put them in the pouch of his shepherd's bag and, with his sling in his hand, approached the Philistine."

David gets his first taste of the loneliness of leadership in this place. No one watches him down at the creek bank. His oldest brother can't stand to see the tragedy unfolding, so he looks away. Later, he knows, he'll have to tell his father how his youngest son took on a suicidal mission or else share a secret of cowardice with his youngest brother. King Saul already feels like a failure, sitting there on his hillside of terror. He hopes the boy won't add a military version of child sacrifice to his résumé. He looks the other way, hoping the boy will lose courage and run home. It's understandable to lose courage in this place. Grown men— hundreds of them—have already lost courage. Goliath, the enemy, doesn't realize an attack is being mounted. He's not watching the boy selecting stones. Most of the soldiers have turned their attention back to center stage. They're not watching David, either.

The creek bank is David's, and David's alone.

It took time to find five smooth stones, five just the right size for a slingshot, five that would fly as true as the thousands already slung from David's leather weapon. It took a lot of time.

In the delay, there was time to ask questions—lots of questions. Time to reflect on how he had managed to work himself into a box. There was no way out, and an enemy awaited. There was time for David to decide if he'd really go through with this idea, this prophet-anointed plan that suddenly seemed very, very real, and very, very frightening. The path to being a king would take him through a nightmare.

Go to seminary campuses, and you'll see people who've been to the creek bank. They've wrestled with an invisible God who called them away from security, away from home, to an invisible future. Somehow, as they spent time along the quiet, lonely creek bank, they found a foundation, a heart foundation, that sent them into battle.

Go to a foreign land and look into the excited, yet frightened, eyes of a missionary, called to a strange place by the same God who arranged to move David from the pasture to the battlefield.

Go to a doctor's office and look into the eyes of the Christian patient who just heard the news that shortened the future. She's already at the creek bank, gathering courage for the Goliath-sized battle that's just ahead.

Go to that brand-new business, where the owner has decided to employ godly principles, taking a risk on God with his family's future.

Maybe you don't have to go anywhere or look at any other examples. Maybe you're at the creek bank already, wrestling with a heart-pounding dilemma—and at the same time, with the Bible's promise of God's providing. You've heard it so many times—that God will provide the miracles for those who believe, that no enemy stands before you that can't be beaten in the name of Jesus. Maybe the battle is just a few steps away, and you know that, as soon as you step away from the creek bank, you'll be walking toward the fight of your life. It's a frightening place to be, down at the creek bank.

Your heart-foundation will make all the difference, and how you lead will be determined by your heart. David had given all of his short life to the search for God's heart, and that search had built a sound foundation of faith.

If you've made it a lifetime practice to search for God's heart, you'll find a way, and your leadership will be defined by the action you take. There comes a time, for David and for us, when leadership requires action. For every one hundred people who will talk about what needs to be done, it seems only one will actually *do* what needs to be done.

David found his five stones, took a deep breath, said a prayer, and took a step toward his future. If your pulse rate doesn't go up when you read the words, "Then he . . . approached the Philistine" (v. 40), you haven't put yourself in the picture. You haven't stood center stage behind the closed curtains, waiting for the audience that is waiting on you. You haven't cleared your throat in the living room, ready to tackle the subject that has long waited for the first shot of the battle. It's a stressful thing to approach the Philistine, no matter what your life circumstance is.

Leaders are made, however, by the action they take. Had David run home, he would have disappeared from history. If you run, you'll never know how dependable God can be.

Depending on God

Godly leaders must depend completely on God. David approached with his heart on his sleeve, and what a heart it was. In the midst of great fear, he sees the giant in all his nine-foot-tall, profanity-laced, armored splendor. Still, right there, David praises his God.

> David said to the Philistine, "You come against me with sword and spear and javelin, but I come against you in the name of the Lord Almighty, the God of the armies of Israel, whom you have defied. This day the Lord will hand you over to me, and I'll strike you down and cut off your head. Today I will give the carcasses of the Philistine army to the birds of the air and the beasts of the earth, and the whole world will know that there is a God in Israel. All those gathered here will know that it is not by sword or spear that the Lord saves; for the battle is the Lord's, and he will give all of you into our hands."
> —1 Samuel 17:45–47

There wasn't much time to talk, but in the midst of the battle, when time was precious, David gave the credit for his victory to the Lord four times. And David gave the credit to God up front, *before* the miracle took place.

It's the faith Shadrach, Meshach, and Abednego showed us years later, believing in God to the point of risking their lives. "We would rather die claiming the living God," they told their enemy, "than bow before your pretend god" (see Dan. 3:16–18).

God rescued the three Israelites in the fiery furnace, and God took David's stone and personally buried it inside Goliath's brain. It was a stunning, fatal blow; in moments, the shepherd boy with the empty sling took the big man's sword and made a tall statement for an army that had become God's army again. Quaking Saul wasn't in charge. Too-young David wasn't in charge. Now, finally, God was in charge.

Leadership Will Change You!

The end of this story has an interesting twist. Saul sends for the new hero and meets him again. Can you picture David? He's fourteen, fifteen, maybe sixteen years old, red-faced, with a day's worth of sweat leaving lines across his dusty face and grimy shoulders. He has an enormous sword in one hand—Goliath's sword—and a giant's head entwined in the other hand, held by fingers that have twisted the Philistine's hair for hours.

Transformed by a day in battle, a day in victory, David doesn't flinch when he stands in front of the king.

> As soon as David returned from killing the Philistine, Abner took him and brought him before Saul, with David still holding the Philistine's head.
>
> "Whose son are you, young man?" Saul asked him.
>
> David said, "I am the son of your servant Jesse of Bethlehem."
>
> —1 Samuel 17:57–58

Know what's unusual about that? A few months before, Saul had asked Jesse for the services of his musical son, the youngest one called David. David had spent time with the king at the king's palace. The record of the request comes at the end of the sixteenth chapter, just one chapter removed from the biggest victory Saul's men had ever seen.

It's amazing that Saul wouldn't know this familiar person, the one behind the harp who had soothed his nerves and who already had a fast friendship with his son, Jonathan. But then again, it's not amazing.

Leadership transforms people. Those who will swallow hard at the creek bank and walk toward the battle with confidence will discover the transformation.

Are you ready to be transformed? Trust your heart and lead!

CHAPTER 8

When Enemies Appear

Maybe you know how troubling it is to have an enemy. It's hard for us to form the words in our minds: "Somebody doesn't like *me*? Of all people . . . *me*?"

Perhaps you've lived a charmed life and never had an enemy. Perhaps, however, you're like the rest of us, and somewhere along the way, you've had to deal with a problem person. Maybe you've already worked through it. Maybe you've already made sense of the situation. Perhaps you've already placed the salve of Romans 8:28 on the cut inflicted by a troubling individual. If you've had an enemy in the past, maybe you've already found the peace that follows the storm and already moved past that troubling chapter of life.

But let me promise you something. When you're in the battle, your stomach will be tied up in knots, and you won't pray peacefully, thanking God for every lesson life teaches you.

Ask David. He did all that God asked him to do, and the miracles were all around his life. And quickly—very quickly—he inherited a powerful enemy. If he thought Goliath had been a tough foe,

David hadn't seen anything yet. Now he was about to have a far bigger enemy than Goliath. Yes, David, the teenager with God's hand upon him, found an enemy in the king of Israel. Can you imagine it? The most powerful man in the nation wanted David dead.

What if the president of the United States was suddenly a personal enemy of yours? What if the president ordered the FBI, the Secret Service, and the armed forces to track you down and kill you, and to do it quickly? David didn't have to imagine that kind of trouble. He lived it. It was his stomach that sloshed with the acid of fear, his legs that felt weak from running, his mind that was exhausted from a lack of sleep.

In the span of one chapter of biblical history, the one following the great victory over Goliath, Saul develops a real hatred for the giant-killer. Just to set the stage and to see the enemy develop, let's look at the facts.

- Saul became jealous of David. The Scripture says, "Saul was very angry; this refrain galled him. 'They have credited David with tens of thousands,' he thought, 'but me with only thousands. What more can he get but the kingdom?' And from that time on Saul kept a jealous eye on David" (1 Sam. 18:8–9). The Bible says Saul's anger was a *charah* anger, an anger that flared up suddenly, the way a flame springs violently off a match when the match is first struck.
- Saul throws two spears at David (1 Sam. 18:11).
- Saul became afraid of David because of David's success. Saul saw that the Spirit of God that had once been in his life was now with David (1 Sam. 18:12–15).
- Saul put David in dangerous positions, hoping that David would be killed (1 Sam. 18:13, 17, 21, 25). However, David had success in everything he did, and he gained more and more popularity. Saul's daughter Michal fell in love with David, and they were married.
- The end result? More anger, more hatred from Saul toward the new, younger, more popular leader: "When Saul real-

ized that the LORD was with David and that his daughter
Michal loved David, Saul became still more afraid of him,
and *he remained his enemy the rest of his days* (1 Sam. 18:28–29,
emphasis added).

It must have been a horrible thing to see how anger was raging
through Saul's life. But how much more horrible it would be to
be the person in whom the anger rages! I would much rather be
with David, trying to survive someone else's *charah* anger, than to
be the one held captive by the flaming rage.

Here are three principles for dealing with enemies that I've
wrestled with in my own life, principles that David learned in a
hurry.

*1. For people who search for God's own heart, enemies will be a
natural, painful part of life.*

What could David have done differently to have made Saul a
friend? Nothing. David's loyalty, his heart, belonged to God. It
may have surprised him that Saul would resent that, but it's the
way an unfaithful heart works. Saul hated what he saw in David,
in part because that's what Saul knew was missing in his own life.

Like every other young man or woman chosen by God, Saul
had been given a blank check from Him. I can't shake the impact
of the words from the Bible. "The Spirit of the LORD will come
upon you in power," the prophet Samuel had said to a younger
Saul, at the very beginning of his calling to be king, "and you will
prophesy with them; and you will be changed into a different
person. Once these signs are fulfilled, do whatever your hand
finds to do, *for God is with you*" (1 Sam. 10:6–7, emphasis added).

Every person who claims God's power through Jesus Christ has
the opportunity to be moved and empowered by God. The Holy
Spirit makes it all possible. But, from the moment Saul heard
those words, the choices he made in life determined how God
was able to bless him and empower him.

Saul made some wrong choices. In fact, Saul made a lot of

wrong choices. He neglected his relationship with the Lord in a painful, horrible way. He didn't know how to worship, to pray, to hear the voice of God. He knew nothing of obedience to God's laws, and he couldn't control the desires in his life. He knew nothing of sacrifice. He had been handed a king's throne, and it ruined him. Saul was addicted to himself.

After Goliath, David dominated Saul's palace. The young man was a painful, painful reminder to Saul of what a God-empowered leader was supposed to look like.

If Saul tried to escape in the palace trophy room, he'd see Goliath's sword hanging on the wall. David hung it there. If he tried to get away to the countryside, he'd hear a song that cut him in his jealous gut: "Saul has slain his thousands, and David his tens of thousands" (1 Sam. 18:7). If Saul tried to get away to the ocean for relief, he'd ride past defeated Philistine villages, the ones David had taken. If he tried to spend time with his children, the conversation invariably would turn to David. The intruder was Saul's son Jonathan's best friend, and his daughter Michal was deeply in love with him! If Saul had a meeting of his cabinet, the first reports would be of David's victories in the field.

Everywhere Saul looked, there was David.

Everywhere Saul looked, he saw his own failure. And failing again, Saul focused his anger at David and not at himself. Though there was opportunity for repentance, Saul didn't repent. David was a living message from God that Saul had failed, and the king decided to kill the messenger.

All the days of his life, Saul considered David an enemy. He would spend the rest of his life trying to kill David and seeing that, without any doubt, God's hand was on the new prince of Israel.

We can explain Saul's anger pretty easily, because he is far removed from us. The history is in the Book, and it's easy to see. What's not easy is to place ourselves in David's shoes, to be committed to the Lord and stay committed to Him when we find ourselves face-to-face with an enemy.

Did David know that Saul was dealing with all the frustrating emotions of failure? No, just as you won't know what an enemy is feeling. Could David feel the intense pain Saul felt when the king saw what God had in mind for a godly leader? No, not any more than you can understand why a person in your life has made you the object of his or her anger. Did David realize that Satan had found room in Saul's heart and was distorting all thought in Saul's mind? No more than you will know who next in your path is being controlled by Satan.

For the moment, understand the painful truth. If you have decided to be a person after God's own heart, if you've committed your life completely to the Lord, your life won't be free of enemies. There's no need, you understand, to go out and *make* an enemy! Just be aware that not everyone will jump up and down with joy because you're walking with the Lord. If you live long enough, enemies will be a natural, painful part of life.

2. In dealing with an enemy, exercise great patience.

David resisted the urge and the opportunity to take Saul's life. He had at least two "God-given" opportunities to end Saul's status as an enemy. Do you remember the stories? One is distastefully humorous. Saul is chasing David through the canyons of Israel, in the Desert of En Gedi, in a place called the Crags of the Wild Goats. It's quite a chase, and Saul and his men are right on top of David and his small army. Nature calls, and Saul needs to take a break. He goes into the very cave where David and his men are hiding, and takes, you might say, a rather vulnerable position.

> He came to the sheep pens along the way; a cave was there, and Saul went in to relieve himself. David and his men were far back in the cave. The men said, "This is the day the LORD spoke of when he said to you, 'I will give your enemy into your hands for you to deal with as you wish.'" Then David crept up unnoticed and cut off a corner of Saul's robe.
>
> —1 Samuel 24:3–4

David could have killed Saul, but he didn't. In fact, he was even truly grieved that he had damaged the king's royal robe. David was, in effect, cutting off his general's stars. Even worse, he may have cut the tassels off his prayer robe, as writer Barney Kasdan suggests.[1] It was a great insult, this cutting of the robe, and it sent a powerful message to Saul.

> Afterward, David was conscience-stricken for having cut off a corner of his robe. He said to his men, "The LORD forbid that I should do such a thing to my master, the LORD's anointed, or lift my hand against him; for he is the anointed of the LORD." With these words David rebuked his men and did not allow them to attack Saul. And Saul left the cave and went his way.
>
> Then David went out of the cave and called out to Saul, "My lord the king!" When Saul looked behind him, David bowed down and prostrated himself with his face to the ground. He said to Saul, "Why do you listen when men say, 'David is bent on harming you'? This day you have seen with your own eyes how the LORD delivered you into my hands in the cave. Some urged me to kill you, but I spared you; I said, 'I will not lift my hand against my master, because he is the LORD's anointed.' See, my father, look at this piece of your robe in my hand! I cut off the corner of your robe but did not kill you. Now understand and recognize that I am not guilty of wrongdoing or rebellion. I have not wronged you, but you are hunting me down to take my life. May the LORD judge between you and me. And may the LORD avenge the wrongs you have done to me, but my hand will not touch you. As the old saying goes, 'From evildoers come evil deeds,' so my hand will not touch you.
>
> "Against whom has the king of Israel come out? Whom are you pursuing? A dead dog? A flea? May the LORD be our judge and decide between us. May he con-

sider my cause and uphold it; may he vindicate me by delivering me from your hand."

When David finished saying this, Saul asked, "Is that your voice, David my son?" And he wept aloud. "You are more righteous than I," he said. "You have treated me well, but I have treated you badly. You have just now told me of the good you did to me; the LORD delivered me into your hands, but you did not kill me. When a man finds his enemy, does he let him get away unharmed? May the LORD reward you well for the way you treated me today. I know that you will surely be king and that the kingdom of Israel will be established in your hands. Now swear to me by the LORD that you will not cut off my descendants or wipe out my name from my father's family."

So David gave his oath to Saul. Then Saul returned home, but David and his men went up to the stronghold.

—1 Samuel 24:5–22

The second opportunity came years later, when David was still on the run, still committed to the Lord, still having to deal with his ultimate problem person. Suddenly, David and Abishai, a loyal soldier, stumbled across Saul asleep in the camp, with a spear stuck in the ground right next to Saul's head. As Abishai pointed out, it looked like a God-given opportunity to be rid of an enemy.

David, the man after God's own heart, didn't see it that way. After all, he'd made an oath to Saul never to kill him. Patience, as hard as it must have been, was called for again.

Abishai said to David, "Today God has delivered your enemy into your hands. Now let me pin him to the ground with one thrust of my spear; I won't strike him twice."

But David said to Abishai, "Don't destroy him! Who can lay a hand on the LORD's anointed and be guiltless? As surely as the LORD lives," he said, "the LORD himself will strike him; either his time will come and he will die,

or he will go into battle and perish. But the LORD forbid
that I should lay a hand on the LORD's anointed."

—1 Samuel 26:8–11

As in the first case, David made quite an impact on Saul. He took the spear and the king's water jug as evidence and began a painful conversation with the commander charged with protecting Saul, and a more painful conversation with Saul, who had to apologize again to David. "Is that your voice, David my son?" (1 Sam. 26:17). began the king who was lucky to be alive. And at the end of the apology, the king says to the king-to-be: "Surely I have acted like a fool" (v. 21).

David would have more enemies in his life, but Saul was the biggest. Eventually, like David's other enemies, Saul would die of his own wrong-doing. In the simplest of language, God took care of David's enemies.

Does the lesson mean that we must let all kinds of unjust actions take place and simply pray that one day God will take care of every problem? By no means. It means patience is the virtue we must employ when dealing with enemies. You're not going to have many personal enemies in life (unless you're making them, of course!), and you have to tread carefully.

Remember Jesus' teaching about dealing with problem people inside the church family? According to Matthew 18:15–17, we are to go, one-on-one, to a person we're having trouble with and try to work out a problem. If the problem is solved, the case is closed. If the problem persists or is unresolved, we're to go back with two or three witnesses. If the problem is solved there—and since some neutral parties are involved, it might very well be solved—then the case is closed. If, in time, the problem persists, we are to take the case before the church and deal with it there. If a person continues to be unrepentant of this flagrant sin that has brought such a situation, then, and only then, are we to, as Jesus puts it, "treat him as you would a pagan or a tax collector" (v. 17).

Though we can read the instructions of Matthew 18 in seconds, it takes weeks to work them out, at the very fastest pace.

What will be employed, in the process, will be patience. Cooler heads will have their say. Decisions won't be made in anger, and many, many so called "enemies" can be transformed into allies.

3. People after God's heart will remain focused on the pursuit of God's heart, no matter what enemies do.

David never turned from his appointment as the next king, but he let God dispose of Saul in His own time. As it would happen, the boy anointed king so many years before wouldn't see the death of Saul or his own coronation until he was thirty years old.

That was a long time to have to deal with an enemy, a long time to be patient, to live in caves and on the run, to pray for answers that never seemed to come. As God would have it, David became king at thirty, the same age priests became eligible to work in the temple and the same age as Jesus when He began His earthly ministry. David would begin at thirty, when life had matured him, when hardship had strengthened him, when his metal had been tested, forged, and steeled against whatever life would give him. David had learned a lot of lessons in life, and in the difficult days, he had found a natural resource, a natural source of help. David had learned to turn to God, over and over again.

David the songwriter would pour out his heart through his songs. Consider just one from David in the Bible's songbook.

> For the director of music. To the
> tune of "Do Not Destroy." Of
> David. A *miktam*. When he had
> fled from Saul into the cave.

> Have mercy on me, O God, have mercy on me,
>   for in you my soul takes refuge.
> I will take refuge in the shadow of your wings
>   until the disaster has passed.

I cry out to God Most High,
   to God, who fulfills his purpose for me.
He sends from heaven and saves me,
   rebuking those who hotly pursue me;
   Selah
   God sends his love and his faithfulness.

I am in the midst of lions;
   I lie among ravenous beasts—
men whose teeth are spears and arrows,
   whose tongues are sharp swords.

Be exalted, O God, above the heavens;
   let your glory be over all the earth.

They spread a net for my feet—
   I was bowed down in distress.
They dug a pit in my path—
   but they have fallen into it themselves.
   Selah

My heart is steadfast, O God,
   my heart is steadfast;
   I will sing and make music.
Awake, my soul!
   Awake, harp and lyre!
   I will awaken the dawn.

I will praise you, O Lord, among the nations;
   I will sing of you among the peoples.
For great is your love, reaching to the heavens;
   your faithfulness reaches to the skies.

Be exalted, O God, above the heavens;
   let your glory be over all the earth.

                           —Psalm 57

Did you see the beginning of the psalm? We don't get explanations about every psalm in the Bible's song book, but we get an important one here: When he had fled from Saul into the cave.

Which cave? No one knows, and it's not important. There were dozens of caves and countless sleepless nights, when David wondered why life had been so unfair and why so much time had to be spent on such a foolish pursuit. He had such an unwanted—and unneeded—enemy.

No matter the circumstances, David focused on God. He remembered the goodness of God, the greatness of God, and the faithfulness of God. He was, as the old hymn says, counting his blessings, naming them one by one.

Then he took his harp, his lyre, and started to sing. He sang praise songs. He slapped himself out of the self-pitying slumber and focused on the Lord. By the end of this song, still in the midst of difficult circumstances, still dealing with an unwanted enemy, David is back where he belongs, singing songs of praise to his God.

Is there an enemy in your life today? Can you dare to exercise the patience and the willingness to wait on God, but even in the waiting, to focus on God and not on your enemy? Listen—your enemy might not have control over his or her unhappy state of life, but that doesn't mean you have to take on that bitterness or unhappiness, too. There is joy in counting blessings. There is ecstatic peace and celebration in remembering the heart of God. Don't waste another minute. Keep a wary eye on your enemy, but keep your heart set on God.

CHAPTER 9

A Heart Molded by Hardship

There's a spot in Death Valley called Dantes View, a place that will tell you more about yourself than it will about the landscape of the American West. From a perch on Dantes View you can either look down 282 feet to the lowest spot in the Western Hemisphere, a place called "Black Water," or you can look up and to the west and see Mount Whitney, a peak that rises 14,495 feet above sea level. Mount Whitney is the tallest mountain in California, one of the tallest in the world.

Therefore, from this one spot, you can choose to soak in one of the highest or the lowest points in the world.

Your pick.

David's "Dantes View" was in an area called Adullam. He could have looked down, or he could have looked up. Thank God, he looked up.

Don't we all have something like Dantes View in front of us, every day? I think so. In fact, I'll bet that most of us have spent more than a little time looking down.

More than likely, every business owner has thought it: "If I just had better people working for me, I'd have a better business." Teach-ers say with a sigh, "If only I had better students, I'd be a better teacher." And nearly every preacher in America has said it: "If I only had better people, I could have a better church—I'd be a better pastor!" Of course, the employees, the students, and the churches are usually wishing they had better bosses, teachers, or preachers!

What if David had waited until he had better people with him before he tried to do something great for God?

> David left Gath and escaped to the cave of Adullam. When his brothers and his father's household heard about it, they went down to him there. All those who were in distress or in debt or discontented gathered around him, and he became their leader. About four hundred men were with him.
>
> —1 Samuel 22:1–2

Wait a minute! Did you really read that? Who came to David to be his first group of soldiers? "All those who were in *distress* or *in debt*, or *discontented* gathered around him, and he became their leader."

What a group! Talk about not having the cream of the crop: the distressed—"What are we going to do, what are we going to do . . . David! What are we going to do?"; those in debt—"How are we going to do anything? Have you got any money? We can't go on another day!"; and the discontented—"I'm sick of Saul and his army! Things are going to change, and they're going to change right now. I'm ready to fight, aren't you?"

We don't envy David, but why should we? Very few people are handed the cream of the crop and a straight ride to the top. Ironically, those who are given that route usually don't make it in the character department.

Saul and the Silver Bedpan

Saul was, for starters, a keeper of donkeys, one of the few sym-bols of luxury for his day. Few people had these sturdy animals that could help make a journey across the rugged terrain of Israel. While David was out keeping sheep as a young man, doing a wooly version of blue-collar work, Saul was doing the detail work for his daddy's Mercedes dealership. It was probably hard work, but he never battled bears or lions, and he wasn't very good with a slingshot. He was born, you might say, with a silver bit in his mouth. When Saul was anointed king, it was almost an embarrassment. No king to overthrow, only the smallest of threats on the immediate horizon. Life was handed to him on a silver platter, but the platter turned out to be a bedpan.

Still, Saul had potential. He was tall, handsome, and winsome. He looked like a leader. He was the people's choice for Israel's first king. Samuel anointed young Saul, and miracles began to happen. He got his father's lost donkeys back and, according to 1 Samuel 10:9, "God changed Saul's heart." God wanted to be a part of this boy's life! Immediately, Saul prophesied with the prophets and saw the frightening truth: Something really was happening in his life. He was going to be king!

But young Saul was shy. Courage wasn't part of his heart. Because he hadn't seen any hardship, hardship hadn't molded him. Right off the bat, he decided not to walk by faith. He wouldn't tell anyone that Samuel had anointed him, and Samuel had to find the young man by casting lots (a traditional method also used for finding unknown guilt!) and then digging through the family's baggage, where Saul had been hiding. Amazingly, people didn't mind this suitcased coward becoming king. They cheered for him and sent him home. In time, Saul led an army in a successful battle against the Ammonites, and the days of being king were on.

Unfortunately, Saul's best day in his new office was his first one. He spared the lives of those who had opposed him and worshiped with all Israel. But that seemed to be the end of Saul's efforts at searching for God's heart. Having been handed a kingdom, he fumbled his opportunity to be a godly leader.

In short order, Saul would:

- panic in the prelude to battle and sacrifice a burnt offering that should have been offered by Samuel (1 Sam. 13:7–15). No big deal? God considered it a major offense. From that day forth, the Holy Spirit of God would be searching for a new king, one who would be a man after His own heart. From that lapse in leadership, twenty-four hundred of Saul's soldiers hightailed it for home, leaving Saul with only six hundred unarmed soldiers. Had it not been for his son Jonathan's faith, Saul's army would have been routed. Panic would prove to be a regular pattern in Saul's life.

- prove on a daily basis that he wasn't interested in the things of worship. Case in point? The writer of 1 Samuel thinks it's important to tell us in chapter 14 that Saul built an altar to the Lord. Then he adds the telling postscript: "It was the first time he had done this" (v. 35). That, to me, is one of the most shocking sentences in the Bible. Here the king of God's people, who was anointed by God's prophet and told he would have the Lord with him in all that he did, couldn't find the time, over the years, to build an altar. It was Saul's responsibility to consistently lead in worship, but he rarely did so.

- almost kill his son Jonathan because of a foolish vow he'd made in war (1 Sam. 14:44).

- set up a monument in his own honor (1 Sam. 15:12).

- build his army on human strength, without asking God for His plans (1 Sam. 14:52).

- deliberately disobey a clear order from God to take no plunder or prisoners from the Amalekites and then lie about his intentions. As he spoke to the prophet in 1 Samuel 15, Saul had the gall to claim the unholy plunder was all meant to be a sacrifice for the Lord.

- continue in a downward spiral in his spiritual life, trying to kill David and Jonathan, and finally, consulting a witch in his hour of deepest desperation. A lifetime of impatience with God, a lifetime of cowardly, faithless behavior finally caught up to Saul in the low point of his life.

It may all go back to the beginning of life, when Saul had a childhood blessed with great times. There was no hardship—no David-like battles with lions, bears, or brothers—to mold his heart.

Consider the last week of Saul's life, and watch how quickly Saul gives up on God. He has invested nothing in faith, and now he has no faith foundation on which to fall.

> The Philistines assembled and came and set up camp at Shunem, while Saul gathered all the Israelites and set up camp at Gilboa. When Saul saw the Philistine army, he was afraid; terror filled his heart. He inquired of the LORD, but the LORD did not answer him by dreams or Urim or prophets. Saul then said to his attendants, "Find me a woman who is a medium, so I may go and inquire of her."
>
> "There is one in Endor," they said.
>
> So Saul disguised himself, putting on other clothes, and at night he and two men went to the woman. "Consult a spirit for me," he said, "and bring up for me the one I name."
>
> —1 Samuel 28:4–8

A tragic picture, this silver bedpan tarnished by faithlessness, a life never molded by hardship.

David Down in the Dirt

Down in the dirt, David was becoming a king. In the cave of Adullam, David surveyed his team. These guys weren't much to look at—distressed, in debt, discontented. His brothers were there, and sisters, too. His mother and father were there, but he found safety for them in a nearby country.

It was in the cave, in the dirt like this, where David wrote so many of his songs. When he was hurting, when he was being hunted, David's heart came to the forefront. You can see it quickly in 1 Samuel 23. Saul is running rampant, having just killed eighty-five priests at Nob. It was a nightmare, and David's men are frightened. There's also a battle nearby, where a Philistine army was looting the village of Keilah. The difference of the hearts of David and Saul is in the simplicity of a trusting prayer.

> When David was told, "Look, the Philistines are fight-
> ing against Keilah and are looting the threshing floors,"
> he inquired of the LORD, saying, "Shall I go and attack
> these Philistines?"
>
> The LORD answered him, "Go, attack the Philistines
> and save Keilah."
>
> But David's men said to him, "Here in Judah we are
> afraid. How much more, then, if we go to Keilah against
> the Philistine forces!"
>
> Once again David inquired of the LORD, and the LORD
> answered him, "Go down to Keilah, for I am going to
> give the Philistines into your hand." So David and his
> men went to Keilah, fought the Philistines and carried
> off their livestock. He inflicted heavy losses on the Phi-
> listines and saved the people of Keilah. (Now Abiathar
> son of Ahimelech had brought the ephod down with
> him when he fled to David at Keilah.)
>
> —1 Samuel 23:1–6

David prayed about his direction in life, which is a huge differ-ence compared to what Saul had been doing. Better than simply praying about a tough choice, David *waited* for an answer from the Lord. He didn't move one inch, didn't lift the first sword, until he had an answer from God. When the men asked David if he was sure of God's direction, David prayed again! And David waited again. With the message confirmed, David and his men headed off for a great victory.

And that little side note about Abiathar having the ephod? That's critical. Abiathar was the high priest, and the ephod was one means of determining God's will. With a leader whose heart searched for God, God was suddenly able to speak clearly and forcefully. As David continued his practice of listening to God and faithfully moving forward, God molded the heart of a great leader, of a king.

A Song from the Heart

Perhaps Psalm 142 was written before the people gathered around David. Perhaps it was when he was alone, running for his life, slipping into caves to avoid Saul's headhunters. David could have written it in one of the cliffs and caves that surround the Dead Sea, not very far from his birthplace of Bethlehem. The Dead Sea, just fifteen miles or so from the high plains of Bethlehem, is the lowest point on the face of the earth. Hide in a cave here, and you've hidden near the bottom of the world.

Whenever it was written, those who were desperate, discontented, and distressed all heard it. They were drawn to a man who—when he was so close to the bottom of the world—chose to look to the heights of the heavens.

> A *maskil* OF DAVID.
> WHEN HE WAS IN THE
> CAVE. A PRAYER.

> I cry aloud to the LORD;
>   I lift up my voice to the LORD for mercy.
> I pour out my complaint before him;
>   before him I tell my trouble.

> When my spirit grows faint within me,
>   it is you who know my way.
> In the path where I walk
>   men have hidden a snare for me.
> Look to my right and see;
>   no one is concerned for me.
> I have no refuge;
>   no one cares for my life.

I cry to you, O LORD;
   I say, "You are my refuge,
   my portion in the land of the living."
Listen to my cry,
   for I am in desperate need;
rescue me from those who pursue me,
   for they are too strong for me.
Set me free from my prison,
   that I may praise your name.

Then the righteous will gather about me
   because of your goodness to me.
                     —Psalm 142

Why did David want to be free of Saul? So he could praise the name of God and so that the righteous would gather about him. Who knew that the righteous people God would first gather around David would have so many problems? Discontented, distressed, up to their throats in debt. And yet, with all their faults, this motley crew had enough faith to follow David into tough battles and tough situations. Together, they all found it true—God molds hearts in the dirt, in the tough places. Hardship has a wonderful purpose in life, and hardship helped mold David into a wonderful leader.

What About Your Heart?

More than likely, somebody reading these words is relating to David in his cave, being hunted and hated, wondering what God could possibly do with the mess of a life he or she has woken up with today. Few people who have everything going for them will take time to read pages on the hardening of character.

Could it be that the tough situation you're in today is to prepare you for a victory tomorrow? Could a setback really be a training time, a preparation time?

I've spent my whole life in the South, and in recent years, I've seen the rebirth of cotton as a major cash crop. Decades ago, cotton was king, and the land was covered with acre after acre of cotton plants. At the turn of the century, the boll weevil invaded the South, and community after community suffered the devastating effects of lost cotton crops.

How could anything good come out of such disaster? It was simple. Across the South, farmers burdened with debt and depression started growing other crops. They grew peanuts, soybeans, and corn. They planted more variety, became more adept at changing conditions, and soon became more successful than they had been with cotton-only crops. Today, if you travel to Enterprise, Alabama, you'll see one of the most unusual monuments ever erected. It's a monument to the boll weevil, put there in 1910! The inscription underneath the oversized insect says: "In profound appreciation of the boll weevil and what it has done to herald prosperity." For the South, the hardship of the boll weevil prepared the way for future farming success.

By the end of his life, David would also look back at his own boll weevil experiences and praise God for them. He learned life's most important lessons not when things were going well but when times were tough. He learned the price of sin not on the rooftop of leisure but in the ashes of grief. He learned how to trust God for protection not in the well-armed battles of warfare but when he ran from cave to cave when Saul's soldiers had all the weapons and all the advantages. David found his heart in tough times, and he found a heart that continued to search for God's heart.

What an unusual thought. Perhaps the tough times in life are a great gift. There is a molding of the heart that will happen only when hammered with all the pain, with all the hurt, with all the hardship. There are some lessons you can learn *only* in the classroom of suffering.

If you're there today, pray that God will help you learn the lessons well. And like David, in time, you will.

CHAPTER 10

Guard Your Heart!

When they first started playing professional football in Texas, the Dallas Texans had a rough time of it. The year was 1952, and the team went 1-11. Not a very good year, to say the least. Actually, things were so bad, it was the team's *only* year!

During training camp in Kerrville, Texas, things were pretty primitive. The first time a football bounced off the playing field into the tall grass that surrounded the players, no one wanted to go after the ball. It seems snakes were a problem in the tall grass of Kerrville.

According to the story, Willie Garcia was the team's equipment manager, a man with an almost-broke desire to get all his equipment back. Willie also had a wooden leg. When no one volunteered to go get the ball, Garcia finally shrugged, looked at the players, and said he'd walk into the grass. "After all," he said, "I've got a fifty-fifty chance the snake will go for the wrong leg."

Let's say you've got a heart that's searching for God's heart, and you're breezing through life. Suddenly the ball of temptation bounces in the tall grass of life around you, and you're toying with the idea of wading into Satan's territory. I need to share a great truth with you. Sooner or later, Satan's going to bite your good leg, and it's not going to be pretty.

If you're ever going to be known as a person who has a heart after God's heart, you're going to have to guard your heart. Maybe you remember the familiar strains of Proverbs 4:23, which states: "Above all else, guard your heart, for it is the wellspring of life."

Once again, the story of David among the pages of 1 and 2 Samuel gives us some great examples of this truth. Here are three keys to guarding your heart.

Key No. 1: Guard your heart by finding a close, Christian friend.

When he was still a young man searching for God's heart, with an immature relationship with God, David needed a friend, and Jonathan filled the void. They forged the friendship in the palace, the king's son finding a kindred heart in the God-appointed heir to the throne. David had no idea how badly he needed a friend like Jonathan, but God made sure a friend was available.

Remember the story? Saul was raging with insane jealousy and trying quietly to kill David. In a short time, it would be open season on the boy from Bethlehem. For the first time in his life, David would be running as a fugitive. If not for Jonathan and David's wife, Michal, he'd have never made it out alive.

Has a friend ever saved your life? If not physically, then emotionally or spiritually? There are times when your heart is ready to break, ready to burst with the stress, the pain, the grief. How good it is to find a friend in an hour of great need. A friend like Jonathan will do whatever it takes to rescue you. What a great spiritual strength Jonathan was! David, with a heart that was searching for God's heart, also needed a friendship with another whose heart belonged to God.

A glimpse into this friendship is like a glimpse into your greatest friendship. We'll pick up the story after David is already running, already convinced that Saul desires him dead. Then he searches for his friend, Saul's son Jonathan.

> Then David fled from Naioth at Ramah and went to Jonathan and asked, "What have I done? What is my crime? How have I wronged your father, that he is trying to take my life?"
>
> "Never!" Jonathan replied. "You are not going to die! Look, my father doesn't do anything, great or small, without confiding in me. Why would he hide this from me? It's not so!"
>
> —1 Samuel 20:1–2

If you read the words with imagination, you read the intensity that was there. It's the same kind of heat that a couple will express in an argument when the stress level is high. It's a delicate time for a friendship, a time that tests the limits of a friend's love. Jonathan gets a blast of David's stress, and David wonders whose side his friend is really on. After all, it is his father who is making David's life miserable.

They set up a meeting, and Jonathan digs for the truth. In two days, he meets David secretly and confirms his friend's fears. He knows his father wants to harm David, and so he sends him away. And there occurs one of the most tender scenes in the Bible.

> After the boy had gone, David got up from the south side of the stone and bowed down before Jonathan three times, with his face to the ground. Then they kissed each other and wept together—but David wept the most.
>
> Jonathan said to David, "Go in peace, for we have sworn friendship with each other in the name of the Lord, saying, 'The Lord is witness between you and me, and between your descendants and my descendants forever.'" Then David left, and Jonathan went back to the town.
>
> —1 Samuel 20:41–42

Why did David weep the most? Perhaps his stress level had finally broken. Perhaps he knew that he'd have to leave his friend and rarely see him again. Perhaps it was the simple, overwhelming fact that he had finally *found* the depth of this man's friendship. Here was a man willing to risk his life for David, a man ready and willing to give up all that was his for David's behalf.

It's a rare discovery to find a friend like that. If you've got one, don't waste a moment. Tell her, tell him, on a regular basis, what she or he means to you. Cherish that friendship. For the rest of David's life, he'd never see a friendship like this again. The day quickly came when David could no longer tell Jonathan what a great friend he was.

Having a godly friend is a great way to guard your own heart. In the presence of a friend, temptation isn't nearly the enemy it is when you're alone. Knowing that you're going to see your friend and talk to your friend is often enough to keep you walking in a right manner. It's a great help in searching for God's own heart.

Immediately on the heels of David's separation from Jonathan, things get a little crazy. In fact, we're about to read one of the most unusual passages in 1 Samuel. As I think about the words that follow, I wonder if David's confusion can be traced back to his separation from his friend. Without his friend, David's faith, David's integrity, was at great risk. His compromises would start immediately, as soon as he arrived at Nob.

So having a great friend isn't nearly enough. You're going to have to have your own relationship with the Lord and your own communion with Him. There is no substitute for knowing God and building that relationship up day after day, which is the second step in guarding your heart.

Key No. 2: Guard your heart by dwelling in the presence of God.

As he ran to the north, David found himself at Nob. Just a short distance from Jerusalem, this was the city where the tabernacle was. There were eighty-six priests in Nob, along with the sacred ephod, a device often used to determine the will of God. As they had done for centuries, the priests of Nob took twelve loaves of bread to the tabernacle every day. Fresh bread replaced the old bread, and the priests were the only ones allowed to eat this very symbolic kind of bread. It was, as the priest said, "consecrated." It was set aside for God. The name of this bread is very important. It was the bread of the Presence.

> David went to Nob, to Ahimelech the priest. Ahimelech trembled when he met him, and asked, "Why are you alone? Why is no one with you?"
>
> David answered Ahimelech the priest, "The king charged me with a certain matter and said to me, 'No one is to know anything about your mission and your instructions.' As for my men, I have told them to meet me at a certain place. Now then, what do you have on hand? Give me five loaves of bread, or whatever you can find."
>
> But the priest answered David, "I don't have any ordinary bread on hand; however, there is some consecrated bread here—provided the men have kept themselves from women."
>
> David replied, "Indeed women have been kept from us, as usual whenever I set out. The men's things are holy even on missions that are not holy. How much more so today!" So the priest gave him the consecrated bread, since there was no bread there except the bread of the Presence that had been removed from before the LORD and replaced by hot bread on the day it was taken away.
>
> —1 Samuel 21:1–6

Apparently, David was starving. He lied to the priest! Saul had assigned no mission to David. Did you notice that the priest was trembling when he met David? This David had turned into quite an intimidating man, able now to take Goliath's huge sword and wield it well. On the one hand, we read these words with disappointment, for David compromised his integrity when under stress. On the other hand, this proved to be an important event. It was somewhat symbolic that David ate the bread meant only for priests. For in time, as king, David would do what God wanted a king to do. David would lead the nation in worship.

The Bible seems to be telling us that it doesn't take a professional minister to lead others in worship. Fathers and mothers need to lead in worship at home, people in businesses need to draw attention to God in the workplace, students need to speak up for the Lord at school, and kings and national leaders need to speak boldly for God as they lead their countries.

Later in life, David didn't hesitate to lead his nation in worship, and all those around him saw that the presence of God was in his life. They all saw that David had invested much of his life in the search for God's heart.

Eating a few loaves of bread may not seem like much, but it was a major event. Years later, Jesus would mention it. At the time, Jesus was arguing with some religious leaders who piously guarded all their rules and regulations. They were very protective of their bread, the bread of the Presence.

> [Jesus] answered, "Haven't you read what David did when he and his companions were hungry? He entered the house of God, and he and his companions ate the consecrated bread—which was not lawful for them to do, but only for the priests. Or haven't you read in the Law that on the Sabbath the priests in the temple desecrate the day and yet are innocent? I tell you that one greater than the temple is here. If you had known what these words mean, 'I desire mercy, not sacrifice,' you would not have condemned the innocent. For the Son of Man is Lord of the Sabbath."
>
> —Matthew 12:3–8

On another day, Jesus would use a stronger illustration:

> Then Jesus declared, "I am the bread of life. He who comes to me will never go hungry, and he who believes in me will never be thirsty."
>
> —John 6:35

On a day when David was away from his close friend for the first time, David was hungry. I believe that in his heart, he was hungry, and thirsty, for a companion. Whether he knew how to put it into words, he needed Jonathan, whose heart also longed for God. At an even deeper level, David needed a real, personal, vivid relationship with God. He needed to have a deep friendship, a vibrant relationship, with God.

Without the presence of a friend, without the security of a mature relationship with God, David wasn't where he needed to be. His integrity had dropped significantly, even to the point of lying. Yes, David had slid from the confident young man who had dropped a giant a few years before.

If you're going to search for God's heart, you're going to need a lot of help. You're going to need the bread of Presence, the Bread of Life, present in your life, every day. It's too important to neglect, even for a day.

That's why reading the Bible is so important. A daily habit of reading the Bible will give you a good diet of confidence, a constant reminder that you're *not* alone. You fight the good fight with supernatural help. That's why it's important to spend a lot of personal time in prayer. And that's why it's critically important to be in a church family. We gain strength when we surround ourselves with the Jonathans of life. The greatest friends you'll ever find are the ones you'll find in God's house. After all, they're the ones searching for the very heart of God!

Key No. 3: Guard your heart by remembering the power of God in the midst of trouble.

It wasn't enough for David to have been anointed king by Samuel, and it wasn't enough for him to have already seen God's miraculous power at work in his life. David was finding, through trial and mostly error, that he'd have to spend the rest of his life guarding his heart.

Soon enough, David's escape leads him to Gath, a small Philistine country just outside the borders of Saul's Israel. He is captured and brought before the king of Gath. Remember David and Goliath? Big man, small kid, giant God? If you compare the pictures of David standing before Goliath and David standing before the king of Gath, you'll get quite a contrast!

Before Goliath, David the teenager was standing tall, rushing toward the giant, proclaiming his faith in a giant-killing God. In a few moments, he was smiling at the stunned Israeli troops, holding the giant's head with blood dripping from the big man's own sword.

Before the king of Gath, it was wads of spit dripping, and it was coming off David's beard. What a scene! A twenty-something David ran from door to door, scratching the door frames with his fingers, falling to the floor, rising again to rush another door frame. The sounds he made must have been full of grunting, growling, and wild-eyed screaming.

There's more to the story than meets the eye. David was playing a trump card. The people in Gath were more than a bit superstitious, and they were especially terrified of madmen. And so David pulled off the acting role of the year, and he escaped with his life.

> David took these words to heart and was very much afraid of Achish king of Gath. So he pretended to be insane in their presence; and while he was in their hands he acted like a madman, making marks on the doors of the gate and letting saliva run down his beard.
>
> Achish said to his servants, "Look at the man! He is insane! Why bring him to me? Am I so short of madmen that you have to bring this fellow here to carry on like this in front of me? Must this man come into my house?"
>
> David left Gath and escaped to the cave of Adullam.
> —1 Samuel 21:12–22:1

Wait a minute. Wasn't the same God who buried a boy's stone in Goliath's head able to get David out of this jam? Certainly. But there's a huge difference in where David is now and where he was when he faced Goliath. This time, David is *alone*. There is no friend standing nearby and no Israelites on the hill to remind him, by their very presence, that God is the God of Israel. Instead, David is "very much afraid" and was shaken to the core. He had lost his soul mate, and he wasn't mature enough to walk with God by himself. Not yet. It was a dangerous place for David to be. Gath wasn't the dangerous place—a place called *Alone* was the place of danger.

If there's ever a time to guard your heart, it's when you're alone. No man or woman, no teenager, is strong enough spiritually to take alone-time for granted. Temptation will leap out at you the way a prowling lion looks for a loner at the back of the pack. A man who never thinks about pornography will suddenly see it on the newsstand or on his pay-per-view TV while he's on a road trip. A woman who would never become drunk at home will suddenly think about it when she's by herself on business.

You'd better watch out when you start playing with temptation. Before you know it, temptation will leave you, like David, with spit all over your face.

Playing with Fire

A few years ago fire-walking was all the rage in parts of the United States. Mystical-speaking fire-walkers from the Middle East and Asia were unloading truckloads of hot coals and an even hotter pop psychology for Americans ready to lose both their cash and their inhibitions.

In one setting, a twenty-foot-long trench of hot coals was prepared. The trench was several inches thick, with a surface temperature of about eight hundred degrees and an interior temperature as high as twenty-five hundred degrees. Then, without the aid of ointments or chemicals being applied to his bare feet, the fire-walker walked across the coals. Every time he performed the amazing feat (pardon the pun), he took exactly four steps in 4.5 seconds. As amazed patrons gasped, the guru crossed the pit up to four times without the slightest trace of his skin being burned or blistered.

The pop-psychology was dished out in a three-day seminar, and at the end of the big weekend, the bravest participants walked across the fire, leaving a world of fears and inhibitions behind them. People paid a lot of money to do this—sort of a version of getting burned without getting burned, if you know what I mean.

But what about the reality of it? How is it possible to walk on hot coals and not be burned? It's really no mystery. It's common knowledge among magicians that the human body can stand short contacts with intense heat without any ill effect. If you're quick enough (please don't try it!), you can actually place your hand in a vat of molten lead and remove it with all your original fingers still intact—and unharmed. Maybe you've passed your hand over a lit match or snuffed out a candle with your fingers. If so, you know the truth. As long as you don't hang around too long, the fire won't hurt you.

As for fire-walking? It's been found that anyone can take four steps across a bed of coals without being burned—but no more than four. Any attempt to take a fifth step will result in immediate and severe burns.

What's the point? It's more than likely that many of God's people, people who really want to search for God's heart, have deviated just a little bit from the search. Maybe they've lost a Jonathan, and that close friendship, that accountability, is gone. Maybe they've found themselves alone, and it's down to a battle of integrity, and integrity isn't winning every fight. Maybe they're just young in the faith, and the presence of God isn't as strong as it needs to be to survive the battle.

How many steps across the hot coals of temptation have you taken? One? Two? Three? Four? Have you lost count? Sooner or later, whenever you hit that fifth step, you're going to get burned and get burned badly. Take today to refocus your walk with God. Pray to God that He'll give you a friend like Jonathan and give you that friend quickly. Pray that God's presence will be as real to you as the bread of the Presence was a real answer to David's physical hunger. And if you've walked across a few hot coals, get off. Right now.

CHAPTER 11

The City of Crisis

Ziklag was a great place to raise kids. It was off the beaten path and always would be. This was the kind of one-stoplight town where you could charge things at the drugstore, and where the gas station attendant coached your kids in Little League on Saturdays. It wasn't unusual to have a pecan pie on your kitchen table when you returned home from church, for no one locked their doors in Ziklag, and people were prone to drop off pecan pies for their neighbors. There would always be big crowds for the annual elementary school play and big turnouts for the volunteer firemen's chicken-dinner fund-raiser every fall. And though they worked hard, few folks in Ziklag ever punched a time clock. People here tended to drive pick-up trucks to work and stop right in the middle of the day for a cup of coffee at the corner café.

This is where David lived. He was a young man full of promise, who knew how to worship with his whole heart. His life hadn't yet been contaminated with wealth, power, or fame. He would often fire up the grill for holiday barbecues and family get-togethers.

He loved the way this small town worked. David loved returning to Ziklag after his work had taken him on the road.

Never mind, for a moment, that this is one of David's more unusual periods of life. Instead of working for God's country, he is now employed by a Philistine king. He fights for the enemy, and he fights well. His reward is an entire town—the tree-lined streets of Ziklag. Forget, if you can, David's story. Just imagine that this is your town. It's where you park your minivan under your carport, where you watch your favorite TV show on Thursdays, and where you attend high school basketball games on winter Friday nights.

It's a place called home.

Try to imagine the day when you come home to disaster.

> David and his men reached Ziklag on the third day. Now the Amalekites had raided the Negev and Ziklag. They had attacked Ziklag and burned it, and had taken captive the women and all who were in it, both young and old. They killed none of them, but carried them off as they went on their way.
>
> When David and his men came to Ziklag, they found it destroyed by fire and their wives and sons and daughters taken captive. So David and his men wept aloud until they had no strength left to weep. David's two wives had been captured—Ahinoam of Jezreel and Abigail, the widow of Nabal of Carmel. David was greatly distressed because the men were talking of stoning him; each one was bitter in spirit because of his sons and daughters. But David found strength in the LORD his God.
>
> —1 Samuel 30:1–6

Maybe you read the story quickly, without feeling the emotion. Maybe you breezed past the heartache, the agony, the crisis. Can you possibly feel the tightness in your chest that David felt? His two wives, gone. Children, gone. House burned to the ground. Corner drugstore a raped pile of rubble. God only knows the evil that has happened to their daughters. The men around him are screaming in grief, each finding his own home destroyed, his own wife, his own children, missing. Some of them are so wild with grief, they are ready to kill anyone, *right now*. David looks like a good target.

We cannot relate to the City of Crisis until Ziklag becomes our destroyed home. It's different when the policeman says that it's your child in trouble. It's different when the doctor is holding a manila folder with your name on it, and the news inside the folder makes him frown. It's different when the funeral director asks you to sit in the front row of the funeral home chapel. It's different when the layoff has your name on the jobless list. It's different when the parents telling their child that a move is necessary are your parents.

What are you going to do in a Ziklag crisis? I can promise you something. Your heart will make the difference. And I'll make you another promise. Your search for God's heart will intensify a thousand times over when you come to the City of Crisis. If you have made this search for God your search, finding God will no longer be an option for sleepy Sunday mornings inside a quaint church sanctuary. Once you arrive in the City of Crisis, the search will suddenly be a gasping, burning, life-dependent desire for air when you're still ten feet below the surface of a lake.

Returning Home to Ziklag

It was a Thursday when I returned home to Ziklag. All I had to do to arrive in the City of Crisis was wake up from a short night's sleep.

My wife, Melody, was a beautiful version of twenty-four. She was in the first stages of pregnancy, with our second child on the way. We had a lovely, smallish country home covered by shade trees and an expansive lawn. I was climbing ladders in a newspaper career, enjoying a lazy, comfortable existence. We had work during the week, friends over on weekend nights, and church on Sundays. Two children would make our family portrait complete, and the pictures would collect dust until someone read my obituary in the distant—far distant—future.

Melody was in trouble from the first moment she awakened. A frantic trip to the hospital went quickly from an emergency room to the halls of an intensive care waiting room. There were hushed conversations with serious doctors, who told me my wife of five years was dying of a stroke.

Immediately, there was a crowd in Ziklag. My pastor was there. My parents and my wife's parents were by my side. Family came from every direction. Friends filled every corner of the waiting room.

But the one presence I needed most was the presence most noticeably absent. My soul was screaming the question my mouth could not speak: *"Where in the world is God?"*

I didn't deserve this. My wife, my child, didn't deserve this. Look at what we'd done! I sang in the church choir. I taught boys in Sunday school every week. As a couple, we had worked with teenagers on Sunday nights. We were faithful in attending church, in giving to church, in making sure we hadn't embarrassed our church. Hadn't the dues we had paid been enough to avoid Ziklag?

Intensifying the Search

King Saul had faced times like this, the worst coming when he and his sons were trapped in battle, a battle that had turned against them with an ICU-waiting room desperation. His pastor—Samuel the prophet—had died, and Saul was horribly alone.

> The Philistines assembled and came and set up camp at Shunem, while Saul gathered all the Israelites and set up camp at Gilboa. When Saul saw the Philistine army, he was afraid; terror filled his heart. He inquired of the LORD, but the LORD *did not answer him* by dreams or Urim or prophets. Saul then said to his attendants, "Find me a woman who is a medium, so I may go and inquire of her."

"There is one in Endor," they said.

So Saul disguised himself, putting on other clothes, and at night he and two men went to the woman. "Consult a spirit for me," he said, "and bring up for me the one I name."

—1 Samuel 28:4–8, emphasis added

For today, forget all the other details of what had happened to Saul. The details of his crisis are as different from David's as your crisis is from mine. The lesson the Bible teaches has to do with the heart of Saul, the heart of David, the heart of me, and the heart of you.

I'll say it again: The search for God's own heart will intensify in a crisis. Saul was desperate for God, and he prayed to God. But there was a delay. Was God waiting to see what kind of faith this faithless king would display? Had God grown callous to a man who had walked further and further away from Him? Was God not amused by the desperate, frantic, emergency-lights-flashing prayer life of a man who never found time for the things of God except when he dialed 911?

Whatever was in Saul's heart, God didn't have to wait long to see it. Before the paragraph of Saul's prayer to God was over, the king was asking for a 1-900 number for a psychic hotline. He found one and called her. He disguised himself, calmed down, and trusted a fake.

Strangely enough, Saul got what he asked for. The psychic called up Samuel, the dead preacher, and Samuel gave him a blistering reproach. When we next hear of this king with the hollow heart, Saul was dead—but his search for God had died long before. He had gone to God with a "Plan B" in his mind, and God simply does not respond to anyone who comes to Him without total, unadulterated submission and dependence.

When you arrive at the City of Crisis, you don't have a lot of time to react. Like Saul, David, and me, you'll fall on your knees and pray. Perhaps you've already been there, and you remember it well. Perhaps, like Saul, like David, like me, you had less than twenty-four hours to find God. It seems unfair, in a way. You spend your whole life going through the routine, and suddenly the Philistines have you surrounded, and the search becomes a matter of life-or-death spiritual survival.

Throwing Out "Plan B"

It was in such a crisis that Saul prayed. But Saul got up after a short time of silence and tried another solution. He gave up on a silent God. David, on the other hand, showed us the core of a man who was after God's own heart. Did you see it? Ziklag was burned to the ground, the wives and children gone for three days, leaving only a trail of children's toys and women's lingerie that disappeared over the horizon. Half the men were crying in the ashes, the other half were listening to the plans to lynch their leader. It was a crisis of immense proportions. It was, certainly, the biggest crisis David had faced up to that point in his life.

"But," says the Bible, "David found strength in the LORD his God" (1 Sam. 30:6). How long did it take to find God? Maybe minutes. Maybe hours. Time is not the factor. The fact is that David didn't have a second option in the back of his mind. He had no "Plan B." It did not occur to him to consult a witch, a counselor, popular opinion polls, or a political advisor. His only hope was God.

Within a few days, David and his men had their lives back together. Wives and children were all home and unharmed. Ziklag was rebuilt, and David was on his way to becoming a king.

But just as it does today, everything hinged on the moment of despair in the City of Crisis. While Saul turned to a witch, David stayed with the Lord.

It sounds simple, until it's your wife in the ICU prison, surrounded by stumped doctors. I prayed all day long. I prayed with my pastor, with my family, with friends, with myself. But there would come a moment, near the midnight of that nightmarish day, when it all came to a head. The games were all over. The Sunday school lessons were just pieces of paper drawn from a book of tradition. The church was a place of regular gatherings, a convenient place to find friends, to bury grandfathers, and to seal marriages.

If God was real, I would find Him at midnight, in the City of Crisis. If He was not real, I would make that horrible discovery in the very hour I needed Him most, more than I had ever needed Him before. Everything I had believed for a quarter of a century hung in the balance. This thing called religion was either going to be the greatest reality ever known to mankind or the greatest farce, the greatest joke ever pulled over the eyes of a stupid world.

In the midst of the midnight prayer, I, too, was completely alone. If you've not been there yet, chances are, you will be. Finally, in the quietness, God began to speak to me. He spoke through a Bible story. Now there are thousands of stories in the Bible, and I hadn't been reminded of any of them on that Ziklag Thursday. But then, at midnight, in complete quietness, there was the story of Paul and Silas floating through my mind. It is not one of the Bible's most familiar stories. But the urging of the story was so persistent, so intense, that finally I gave up my prayerful begging and tried to remember the story of Paul and Silas.

According to the New Testament record of early church history, Paul and Silas, itinerant preachers, had landed in Philippi. It was a beautiful place, slightly larger than David's Ziklag. The ministry there was sweet and consistent. By and large, folks tolerated the two men and their message about a Messiah named Jesus. A few were believing and meeting on a regular basis.

Then came the miracle. A child was healed! Paul and Silas had performed the miracle in the name of Jesus, and there was amazement around the city. However, the tide turned quickly against the preachers. They had not just healed a child, they had stopped a small business. The girl had been an adolescent psychic, a carnival-child curiosity. The adults who owned this slave-child had made a small fortune on her. Now they'd have to find another way to pay for the second car she had afforded them. They concocted a story and drummed up false charges against the strangers.

Paul and Silas were arrested, beaten, and thrown in jail. I could remember most of the details through the fog of that hospital night, and I related to the two men. They had been punished for doing good. They were held in a dungeon of despair for serving the very God who should keep them out of such places. Still, it seemed strange that I would be recalling a Bible story at all.

And it was then, right then, that God spoke clearly. He spoke through the verse that had drifted by me through years of church attendance. I had heard the sermons, read the story, and ignored the meaning. The impact, I have since discovered, could only be found in the City of Crisis.

> About midnight Paul and Silas were praying and sing-ing hymns to God, and the other prisoners were listen-ing to them.
>
> —Acts 16:25

God wanted me to sing? God wanted praise, worship, adora-tion—while I was spitting the bitter ashes of Ziklag out of my mouth?

Yes, He did.

It was hard to start, horribly hard. All that was human in me wanted to avoid praise in the midst of pain. How could I tell God how wonderful He was when He had dropped me off at the gates of hell?

Nevertheless, I finally agreed to try. The prayer began with a simple praise of nature, of God's creation. Once begun, it was easier than I had imagined. Soon, I was caught up in thanksgiving over life, over family, over my wife's life, over my daughter, over this child in my wife's womb.

I cannot put down on paper what happened next. It's simply impossible to describe meeting God. My search in the City of Crisis had brought me to the throne room of heaven. The keys of praise, thanksgiving, and worship had unlocked my heart to see that God was ready to take the burden from me. My request was simple. "God," I prayed, "the doctors don't know what to do, and I don't know what to do. My wife belongs to You. I give this whole situation to You."

And it was over. The tension, the crisis, the fear—it was finally all gone. When Paul would write those same believers at his beloved church in Philippi years later, he would remind them of the peace that passes all understanding, a peace that defies all comprehension (Phil. 4:7). Those Philippians would remember Paul's prison ordeal, the earthquake that followed, the opened prison doors, the prison guard's family that all came into the church after the miracle of Paul's midnight song service. Their lives were forever changed by that one event, all changed because of Paul's prayer of praise in the midst of his pain.

I will always remember the midnight earthquake of my soul. It was an earthquake that shook me with the reality of God. What a thought—a real God! And there was a stunning peace that flooded my young-husband's heart with a trusting sleep.

In the midst of my spiritual miracle, a doctor woke me with the news that my wife had pulled through the crisis with a physical miracle. Over the next six months, my wife and I both would need that same miraculous peace as we endured two bouts of brain surgery, several slow weeks of rehab, and a nervous Good Friday morning when a second daughter was born healthy, bald, and more beautiful than I had ever imagined.

I would need God's presence simply to learn that the greatest miracle of all was not finding a happy ending to every Ziklag story, but of learning that God is real. It's so true—God desires a living relationship with us that far surpasses the religion of men or the circumstances of life.

Ziklag is still a beautiful town. The beauty, however, has a special depth on this side of trouble. There's more there than tree-lined streets and children playing on school playgrounds. In Ziklag is the memory of the crisis and the remembrance of the reality of God. It is remembering the miracle of peace right in the center of the nightmare.

Have you found yourself in Ziklag, the City of Crisis, recently? Your choice is amazingly simple and profoundly difficult. Like Saul, you can turn away from God. Or like David, you can turn toward God with trust and praise.

My message is simple. No matter the circumstances, grief, heart-ache, or pain, turn without reservation and trust the Lord your God. Praise Him in your heart, and you will discover that God richly rewards those who search after God's own heart.

CHAPTER 12

A "Prime-Time" Search
for God's Heart

Talk about a man who didn't realize what he had. There's the story of a man who was traveling through the countryside when one of his tires blew out. As he fumbled with the jack, he heard someone comment, "That trip to Japan was wonderful last spring." The man with the flat stood up but didn't see anyone. However, there was a horse nearby peering over the pasture fence. Sensing the heat was causing him to hear things, he bent back down and started working with the lug nuts.

He heard the voice again, and he quickly turned around. As he did, the horse looked at him and said, "Yes, that trip to Japan was almost as good as the one to Paris and Rome the year before." The man became hysterical with excitement. He rapidly fixed his tire and drove up to the farmhouse. He pulled out his wallet and told the farmer, "I'll buy that old horse in the meadow for any price."

"Awe, shucks, you don't want that horse," said the farmer. "Why that old horse hasn't been to half the places he talks about."

That old farmer didn't realize what he had! And neither do some of us. Right in the prime of life, many people are always waiting on some future event, some better time, or some perfect set of circumstances before they'll find happiness or contentment.

And all the while, they've got a talking horse in the meadow.

The best years of your life might be going on right this moment! Let's take a look at David's life in his best years. At this point, he is king—a good king—and he was avoiding the temptations that would soon bring his life to a crashing halt.

In the course of time, David defeated the Philistines and subdued them, and he took Metheg Ammah from the control of the Philistines.

David also defeated the Moabites. He made them lie down on the ground and measured them off with a length of cord. Every two lengths of them were put to death, and the third length was allowed to live. So the Moabites became subject to David and brought tribute.

Moreover, David fought Hadadezer son of Rehob, king of Zobah, when he went to restore his control along the Euphrates River. David captured a thousand of his chariots, seven thousand charioteers and twenty thousand foot soldiers. He hamstrung all but a hundred of the chariot horses.

When the Arameans of Damascus came to help Hadadezer king of Zobah, David struck down twenty-two thousand of them. He put garrisons in the Aramean kingdom of Damascus, and the Arameans became subject to him and brought tribute. The LORD gave David victory wherever he went.

David took the gold shields that belonged to the officers of Hadadezer and brought them to Jerusalem. From Tebah and Berothai, towns that belonged to Hadadezer, King David took a great quantity of bronze.

When Tou king of Hamath heard that David had defeated the entire army of Hadadezer, he sent his son

Joram to King David to greet him and congratulate him on his victory in battle over Hadadezer, who had been at war with Tou. Joram brought with him articles of silver and gold and bronze.

King David dedicated these articles to the LORD, as he had done with the silver and gold from all the nations he had subdued: Edom and Moab, the Ammonites and the Philistines, and Amalek. He also dedicated the plunder taken from Hadadezer son of Rehob, king of Zobah.

And David became famous after he returned from striking down eighteen thousand Edomites in the Valley of Salt.

He put garrisons throughout Edom, and all the Edomites became subject to David. The LORD gave David victory wherever he went.

—2 Samuel 8:1–14

Prime-Time Years Take Time

At times I'm quite impatient. Do you ever get impatient? Maybe the next time we're tapping our fingers waiting on a slower-than-usual microwave oven, or a printer that doesn't laser-jet the pages quite fast enough, we should remember Walter Shane's family. The Shane family lives on St. Paul Island in the Bering Sea in Alaska. Let's say the Shanes want a pizza. They do all the things my family does when the menu calls for a delivered pizza. They argue over the toppings, settle on the ones they usually get, and call the pizza joint. They get the amount of money ready, along with $23 for shipping charges, and then sit down for a rather lengthy wait. Why, if the weather is good and the flight isn't canceled, that pizza will be delivered in just three days!

David waited a long time for his favorite pizza to finally land on his plate. The passage we just read from 2 Samuel 8, begins with a tantalizing phrase: "In the course of time . . ."

Do you know how much time it took David to reach chapter 8?

It takes us only a matter of minutes to read his life's story and only a second or two to read that line, but it took David *years* to arrive at chapter 8. Anointed king as a boy, he would be thirty years old before Saul was dead and he was really king. It was another seven years or so before the land was secure and David could breathe the clean air of peace. It was then, after at least twenty-five years, that his prime time began. It was then, you might say, that the house payment was manageable, the kids were well on their way to their educations, and a retirement fund was growing nicely in his broker's downtown office.

There is much value in the passing of years. Are you willing for God to write the words "in the course of time" on your life's story? Please be patient.

Chuck Yeager, the famous pilot who first broke the sound barrier, shared an interesting story in his autobiography. In the late 1950s at Edwards Air Force Base, while another pilot was flying a Mach 2 fighter, he fired some shells from his cannons and then— believe it or not—outraced his own shells and shot himself down![1]

Want to shoot yourself down? Don't exercise patience. Want a successful flight through life? Wait on the Lord and benefit from the prime-time years God has given you.

High school students—please listen. In time, you'll have all the answers. You'll have that mate, perhaps, and direction for life. You'll know a lot more in ten years than you know now, and God will be faithful. College students, young adults, please be patient. When God is ready to direct your path, God will faithfully and clearly do it. Remember that the Bible says that God is not the author of confusion. If confusion reigns over a decision to be made, don't make it! Wait on the Lord and watch His faithfulness.

More than likely, a middle-aged adult, even an older adult, reading these words right now is considering a major change in life. Perhaps the decision concerns work, a career, pursuing more education, or a new living environment. If that's you, please do not forget to pray and commit to waiting on the Lord.

I can remember a time in my own life, just a few years ago, when I would cry out before the Lord begging for His direction in my life. I could sense it. I could feel it. I knew God wanted something for my life other than a career in journalism, yet God was painfully slow in telling me His plan. But God is wise and all-knowing. If God had told me all that would happen to me in the span of a decade, He knew He'd probably be dealing with a young heart-attack victim! Now that the plan is clearer to me, there is peace, joy, and a great clarity to my life's purpose. I rejoice at what God has done, and I want to encourage you to remember that your prime time takes time—lots of time.

Prime-Time Years Are Difficult

I ran across a comment from Jacques Plante, a former standout goalie for the Montreal Canadians. There, in the prime time of his life, in the best physical shape of his life, making the most money he'd ever made, Plante admitted that all of his work wasn't pleasant. After all, said the goalie, "How would you like it in your job if every time you made a small mistake, a red light went on over your desk and fifteen thousand people stood up and yelled at you?"

Tomorrow, at the office, when things are going poorly, remind yourself of Jacques and thank God for no red light over your desk!

In prime time, things were pretty good for David. He was healthy, married to a beautiful wife, his kids played in the new parks in Jerusalem. Life was great all the time, wasn't it?

No, it wasn't. There were some things David had to do, in the course of his job, that just were not pleasant. It doesn't sound like the eight to five grind you might put in, but here are two cases where David did what he had to do. I can't imagine at all that he enjoyed the process.

In the course of war, he put to death two of three Moabites with a nightmarish length-of-cord processing. In the course of war, he hamstrung hundreds of fine horses. They were useless. It was a destructive, difficult process, and it was his job.

Later on, 2 Samuel 8:15 says, "David reigned over all Israel, doing what was just and right for all his people." That means he was enjoying every moment, living happily ever after, doesn't it? No! Have people ever liked a leader who did what was just and right? Have they ever liked the rulings of a judge who ordered compliance with the law? Have they ever enjoyed parking tickets, speeding tickets, or IRS audits? David had to live with intense pressure in his prime time, and at times, that pressure must have been very difficult.

In the prime of your life, whether you're thirty, forty, or fifty, you might really go through days when you dislike your work. You might go through times when you wish you could throw it all away. The grass may look greener on the other side of town, with another job, with other responsibilities. But every job ever created has its downside. Every job available today has its good points, its bad points, and its unbearable points.

Prime-time football players get tackled so hard they lose consciousness. Prime-time baseball players get hit with ninety-miles-per-hour fastballs. Prime-time dancers on Broadway strain muscles to the max and beyond it. Prime-time musicians go on grueling road tours. In your prime time, you'll have some tough work. Sure it can be tough. Even so, don't miss your prime time.

Some years ago, Robert Hastings wrote a nice piece that reminds us of the value of prime time. Listen to the illustration of "The Station."

> Tucked away in our subconscious is an idyllic vision. We see ourselves on a long trip that spans the continent. We are traveling by train. Out the windows we drink in the passing scene of cars on nearby highways, of children waving at a crossing, of cattle grazing on a distant hillside, of smoke pouring from a power plant, of row upon row of corn and wheat, of flatlands and valleys, of mountains and rolling hillsides, of city skylines and village halls.
>
> But uppermost in our minds is the final destination. On a certain day at a certain hour we will pull into the

station. Bands will be playing and flags waving. Once we get there so many wonderful dreams will come true and the pieces of our lives will fit together like a completed jigsaw puzzle. How restlessly we pace the aisles, damming the minutes for loitering—waiting, waiting, waiting for the station. "When we reach the station, that will be it!" we cry. "When I'm 18." "When I buy a new 450 SL Mercedes Benz!" "When I put the last kid through college." "When I have paid off the mortgage!" "When I get a promotion." "When I reach the age of retirement, I shall live happily ever after!"

Sooner or later we must realize there is no station, no one place to arrive at . . . once and for all. The true joy of life is the trip. The station is only a dream. It constantly outdistances us.

"Relish the moment" is a good motto, especially when coupled with Psalm 118:24—"This is the day the LORD has made; let us rejoice and be glad in it." It isn't the burdens of today that drive men mad. It is the regrets over yesterday and the fear of tomorrow. Regret and fear are twin thieves who rob us of today.

So, stop pacing the aisles and counting the miles. Instead, climb more mountains, eat more ice cream, go barefoot more often, swim more rivers, watch more sunsets, laugh more, cry less. Life must be lived as we go along. The station will come soon enough.[2]

What a great illustration! And what a great truth. Prime time won't come at the station, it's all along the journey. Enjoy the days—*now*. Enjoy the children, enjoy your spouse, enjoy your in-laws, enjoy your parents. Enjoy the trips, the visits, the time you can kick back and just watch a ball game. You'd better enjoy it now, because it may never get any better than it is for you, right now.

Prime-Time Years Take Commitment

The success of your best years is directly related to your commitment to God. It is no accident that David succeeded. God gave David success. God won victory after victory for David, because David quickly and consistently gave God the credit.

It had begun for David in chapter 7, when Nathan the prophet received a wonderful promise from God for David.

- *God's promise for David:* fame and a confident future for his family.
- *God's promise for the nation Israel:* a land to call their own, freedom, peace, no wicked, oppressive leaders, and rest from war.
- *God's promise for David's children:* permission to build the temple, a personal relationship with God, punishment for wrongdoings, everlasting love, and an opportunity to be on Israel's throne forever.

David was getting to watch God keep His promises. David had seen God's hand take down a giant called Goliath, and he had been fighting smaller battles for well over a decade. He had survived Saul's manhunts, and he had survived battles with depression. David had seen God at work over and over again.

David loved God so much that he wanted to build the first temple himself. If not for an instruction from the Lord, he would have built the temple. But that job, said the Lord, was to be reserved for his offspring.

God made a lot of promises to David, and it took a long time for all the promises to be completed. To make things complicated, David got distracted by temptation and really slowed down the process. It took time. It still takes time to see the promises of God fulfilled in our lives.

I like what Beth Moore wrote in her study of David.

> When God assures us of a promise, He desires for us to respond by assuming a posture of cooperation in the fulfillment of that promise. At other times, God directs

us to sit still and wait. *Wisdom involves learning to know the difference.*[3]

Do you know the difference? You will, if you commit your heart to God and keep it committed during your prime-time years. Even when you're the strongest, the healthiest, the wisest, the prettiest, the sharpest, the best-paid, and even when you're at the top of the heap (you'd better remember you're still only on top of a heap!), your heart must, absolutely must, stay committed to God.

David was king, but he'd never have made it if he hadn't given his heart to God as a little boy.

David was a great warrior, a champion of champions, but he'd never have seen the glory if he hadn't taken some small steps of faith toward his first giant. God proved faithful that first time, and God remained faithful to David for the rest of his life.

David was a wealthy man, but he wouldn't have been wealthy if he hadn't sung praises to God when he was broke.

David was a clear leader. But in order to lead, he first had to learn how to follow, and he followed the Lord. And when people saw the process, they said of him simply, "This man has a heart after God's own heart."

There's a story going around of a pediatrician who tried to make his check-ups as enjoyable as possible. With one four-year-old girl he looked into her ears and asked, "Do you think I'll find Big Bird in here?" The girl didn't say a word. He then used a tongue depressor to gaze down her throat. This time he asked, "Do you think I'll see Cookie Monster down there?" The girl remained silent. But when the doctor placed the stethoscope to her chest, it was time for the child to set things straight. The doctor asked, "Do you think I'll hear Barney in there?" She replied, "Oh, no! Jesus is in my heart. Barney is on my underwear."

Want to make it in the search for God's own heart? Relegate everything in your life to underwear status and keep Jesus in your heart. Let Jesus direct your path. Listen to his words again, "Seek first his kingdom and his righteousness, and all these [other] things shall be given [in His time] to you" (Matt. 6:33).

CHAPTER 13

Fighting Satan's "Heart Attacks"

While working as a court-appointed attorney, Emory Potter was assigned a client who had been accused of criminal trespass. Mr. Potter probed his client with some general background questions, including if the man had any previous arrests or convictions. The man ashamedly said, "Yes, sir, I've got quite a few." The attorney then asked, "Any felonies?" The man straightened his shoulders and indignantly replied, "No sir! I specialize in misdemeanors!"

So do I. Like a lot of folks, I'm quick to admit I'm in the fold of Romans 3:23—that "all have sinned and fall short of the glory of God"—but I insist on believing my sins almost always fall in a self-described "misdemeanor" category.

Have you been there, too? In the long run, I don't think any of us really want to stand before the Lord God of heaven and insist that our "misdemeanor" sins weren't that bad. Sin is sin, and God can't stand it. But you know what? It's the misdemeanors, the little sins, that often take us to the deadliest places.

Maybe this story is more vivid. In April 1988, a sky diver attempted to film a number of fellow jumpers as they all leaped from the plane and began their free-fall. The jump started off well. If you saw the video, you saw some exciting footage of smiling, exhilarated sky divers and midair stunts. Then there is footage of each sky diver pulling his ripcord, opening his chute, and beginning the slow, lazy float to the earth. But the last segment of the film is one of total chaos. It is here the cameraman makes a horrifying discovery. In his enthusiasm to film the dive, the photographer forgot to put on his parachute!

It wasn't until he reached for the ripcord that he realized his error. Such a small oversight—such a tragic outcome. And what a picture of sin. The jump was an eventful and exhilarating trip for a few fleeting moments. But the end result was death. We might as well admit both sides of the truth. Sin can be exciting for a while—temporarily thrilling—but the end result is death.

Another illustration that works well here is the illustration of a heart attack. Years spent neglecting an exercise program, years of eating unhealthy foods, or years of carrying an inherited disease can cause a sudden, deadly pain that will change your life, and possibly end it.

Satan has another kind of "heart attack." Satan's goal, Jesus said, is to steal, kill, and destroy (John 10:10). Satan's goal is to attack any unguarded portion of your heart, and he'll use every weapon he has to destroy your family, your influence, your joy. Since we're already carrying an "inherited" spiritual genetic makeup of a sinful nature, we've got to be ready to fight Satan's attacks on our hearts. If we don't fight back, the result of such attacks can be as deadly, and as devastating, as physical heart attacks.

Before we move forward, I need to ask you to do four things.

1. *Be patient.* We could spend a lot of time on this portion of David's life. Volumes have been written on David's lowest moment. We're going to spend two chapters here, on what may be the most important message of 1 and 2 Samuel. If

you are searching for God's own heart, you cannot move forward without considering the truths presented in the story of David and Bathsheba.

2. *Be encouraged.* The story of David and Bathsheba is one of the great tragedies recorded in the Bible, but it is also a story of survival. Both David and Bathsheba came to a point of repentance and of living a joyful life again. God was able to do a work of restoration in their lives. If God could restore these two people, he can restore you!

3. *Be open.* Will you honestly open every corner of your life, right now, and let God speak to you? Will you let God clean every corner of your life? Will you be willing to let God remove anything—or anyone—that needs to be removed?

4. *Be in prayer.* These chapters were tough for me to write, and they might be tough for you to read. If you'll stop and pray, God will speak much more clearly than I ever could. God's instructions will be plainer than words on paper. Pray that will happen for you.

Here's how the story develops. David was taking a break, and his life fell apart. He was enjoying a season of—how shall I say this?—laziness. It was here, in the midst of laziness, that David's relationship with God suffered a near fatal blow. David didn't wake up one morning and decide to commit adultery and murder. David didn't decide, over his toast and coffee at the breakfast table, to ruin his standing as a man after God's own heart. No, it was the little things, the misdemeanors, the compromises that suddenly led to a place where the heart attack was about to happen. Here's the Bible's account:

> In the spring, at the time when kings go off to war, David sent Joab out with the king's men and the whole Israelite army. They destroyed the Ammonites and besieged Rabbah. But David remained in Jerusalem.
> One evening David got up from his bed and walked around on the roof of the palace. From the roof he saw

a woman bathing. The woman was very beautiful, and David sent someone to find out about her. The man said, "Isn't this Bathsheba, the daughter of Eliam and the wife of Uriah the Hittite?" Then David sent messengers to get her. She came to him, and he slept with her. (She had purified herself from her uncleanness.) Then she went back home. The woman conceived and sent word to David, saying, "I am pregnant."

So David sent this word to Joab: "Send me Uriah the Hittite." And Joab sent him to David. When Uriah came to him, David asked him how Joab was, how the soldiers were and how the war was going. Then David said to Uriah, "Go down to your house and wash your feet." So Uriah left the palace, and a gift from the king was sent after him. But Uriah slept at the entrance to the palace with all his master's servants and did not go down to his house.

When David was told, "Uriah did not go home," he asked him, "Haven't you just come from a distance? Why didn't you go home?"

Uriah said to David, "The ark and Israel and Judah are staying in tents, and my master Joab and my lord's men are camped in the open fields. How could I go to my house to eat and drink and lie with my wife? As surely as you live, I will not do such a thing!"

Then David said to him, "Stay here one more day, and tomorrow I will send you back." So Uriah remained in Jerusalem that day and the next. At David's invitation, he ate and drank with him, and David made him drunk. But in the evening Uriah went out to sleep on his mat among his master's servants; he did not go home.

In the morning David wrote a letter to Joab and sent it with Uriah. In it he wrote, "Put Uriah in the front line where the fighting is fiercest. Then withdraw from him so he will be struck down and die."

So while Joab had the city under siege, he put Uriah

at a place where he knew the strongest defenders were. When the men of the city came out and fought against Joab, some of the men in David's army fell; moreover, Uriah the Hittite was dead.

—2 Samuel 11:1–17

Before we move on, maybe we should give David some credit. Maybe it was an accident that he saw this beautiful woman bathing. Maybe he, the king of the city, didn't know where women bathed. Maybe. He probably did know, but let's give him the benefit of the doubt. In the course of living, it's possible to see the wrong thing on the Internet, the wrong thing on a television channel, the wrong thing lying beside the road, or some filth that someone used and discarded. It's possible that something like that happened to David. But here's the difference: David backed up, looked around to see if he was alone, and then he returned to inspect what he should not have been watching.

When David broke that one "misdemeanor" rule, when he was willing to step out of his relationship with God, things quickly got worse. The situation steamrolled him. What started out as an "innocent" sin of looking where he should not have been looking—something that we could write off as a so-called "harmless" sin—turns into flagrant sin. He asked who the woman was. Along with learning her name, he also learned that she was one man's daughter and another man's wife. There were danger signs immediately posted around this woman. This was forbidden territory.

But David elected to move forward with the sin. In fact, things move so quickly, it may be more accurate to say that the sin moved him. Once David gave in to the smallest temptation, larger temptations moved in for the kill.

When Bathsheba came back with the positive pregnancy test, David tried to cover up his crime by bringing Uriah home. He gets her husband drunk and encourages him to go home. You can almost hear David: "Hey, Uriah, it's time to relax! Go home and have a great time with your wife. Why don't you take a bath? You'll spot your beautiful wife and just let nature take its course."

Perhaps David thinks: "Who could resist an opportunity to have sex?" The record shows that David certainly can't! He's got multiple wives, a harem full of women, and an insatiable appetite for physical pleasure. But David gets the shock of his life. Uriah is proof that one can have discipline. Uriah even has more discipline as a drunk man than David does as a sober man.

Your Heart, a Target

If you seek to have a heart relationship with God, Satan will constantly seek to attack your heart. Temptation is Satan's tool of warfare, Satan's cholesterol, Satan's blockage of major prayer arteries.

There is a certain madness about cholesterol. For years, the small bits of fat may not stop at all on the blood-rushing trips throughout your body. But sooner or later, one molecule sticks. A small thing, no doubt, but it's there. It's like a single sin in David's life or in your life. Another molecule comes along and sticks beside the first. In time, a pile of fat becomes a heart blocker. In your physical body, the attack on the heart is often silent for years and then suddenly painful beyond description. Such an attack will require tremendous, intensive-care attention for you to survive.

In our spiritual bodies, sin snowballs into a great blockage of the relationship we seek with God. One by one, little by little, the "fat" piles up. Perhaps we start with misdemeanor sins. Eventually, we may graduate to the lying, the murder, the adultery of David's life. But don't miss the point. Once we break the rules of God, once we get over the guilt of the first sin, it's just a little bit easier to sin a second time.

When the sins pile up, a heart attack isn't far away. Satan organizes the attack, orchestrates the temptation, and laughs at our pain on his way to seek a new victim.

For David, a man after God's own heart, it happened very quickly. As quickly as a marriage can dissolve because of a one-night fling. As quickly as a job can be lost because of improprieties at the office. As quickly as a family name can be tarnished because of a David-like lack of discipline. As quickly as the pregnancy test can come back positive and change your entire life.

Over the course of three thousand years, nothing—absolutely nothing—about the nature of sexual sin has changed. Reading this story of David and Bathsheba reminds you, perhaps, of watching a scandalous news story on television or of watching a politician attempt to survive political turmoil because of his own lack of sexual integrity. It may even remind you of personal struggles. May I tell you something you already know? Satan's attacks on our hearts are sneaky, sly, subversive. They are always there. You can fight for years, and you'll come to the same conclusion: You can exercise discipline, but you can't exorcise the demons.

Temptation springs upon you at a moment's notice. As quickly as a billboard flashes past on the interstate. As quickly as a magazine cover smiles at you behind the convenience store attendant. As quickly as the TV channel hits the wrong station at the wrong time, it'll nail you to the wall and take delight in killing you dead.

David is a frighteningly familiar character to us all. It's obvious that he should have never committed the crimes of his heart. He stole another man's wife, then murdered the man. And for the better part of a year, he lied. He lived a lie. He pretended all was normal.

Can you remember young David in the fields around Bethlehem watching his father's sheep, singing songs of praise to God, and risking his life to protect his flock? He was a man of such integrity that not even the giant enemies of God's people could stand in his way.

So how did he wake up one morning to be a sexual addict? How did he come to the point of walking around in secret, looking for scenes of lust? How would he come to the point of such weakened integrity that he would be consumed by lust, act on that lust, and then pretend nothing was wrong?

I'll tell you how he did it. He took it one small step at a time. Just one tiny step of compromise, one tiny movement of wrongdoing—and then another, and then another—until he got accustomed to a life of compromise. From that point on, the winds of sin circled around him like a swirling tornado.

David had a wife, but then he added another wife. Then he added another, and another, and another, and another, and another—seven in all. Seven women ready, frankly, to satisfy his sexual appetite. But seven wasn't enough for David. He had a harem. More women just to meet his needs for physical pleasure. Do you see what that says? David couldn't say no to his sexual urges. His example would be so profound that his sons Amnon and Absalom would follow in his footsteps and imitate his lack of sexual discipline. Later, Solomon would have a cast of one thousand wives and concubines. Like David, Solomon had absolutely no sexual discipline. He learned from his father, who by his very actions said, "Seven wives and a harem are not enough. I'm going shopping for a newer, brighter model." Bathsheba was there, and the tornado of temptation touched down. The heart attack was in a full-blown fury. The destruction that followed was overwhelming.

If you can't say no to temptation, the tornado will touch down in your life, too. The chest pains will start, and the silent spiritual killer will send you to a spiritual grave or, at best, an intensive care unit.

I say it again: If you seek to have a heart relationship with God, Satan will constantly seek to stop you with a "heart attack." There are things we can do to fight for our spiritual health, and one of them is simply being aware of a dangerous area.

A Potent Poison

Pornography is one of the most potent poisons of the heart. If you read the next ten chapters of 2 Samuel, you'll see mass destruction. The murder of Bathsheba's husband. The rape of David's daughter. The murder of David's son. The rebellion and death of another son. A massive, insulting, sexual display on the rooftops of Jerusalem. You'll see civil war and despair. You'll see years and years of defeat. You'll see a loss of zeal for God and more pain than anyone could have possibly imagined.

Know where it all started? Know where it could have all been avoided? It was on one rooftop, when David went to a place, a secret place, where he could look at a naked woman who was not his wife. That, in a very simple definition, is what pornography is. Looking at an unclothed person who is not your spouse. It's not art, it's not free speech, it's not a harmless form of entertainment. It's a favorite weapon in Satan's arsenal, and it is a deadly poison for your heart.

David didn't have *Playboy* magazine, he had this one, secret place. He didn't have video rental stores, he had the women's bathing area. He didn't have a strip bar, he had his own personal viewing area.

If David had stepped back, right at that moment, asked for forgiveness, and literally turned around and left, he could have stopped the whole thing. That would have been a great example of repentance. But he didn't turn away! The attraction was too strong. The pull was too great. And the king known as a man after God's own heart fell to great destruction. Yes, this moment in Scripture is the clearest visual picture of pornography's harm the Bible ever gives us.

Let's take a break for a moment and consider another thought altogether. The pride and joy of Georgia business is surely the Coca-Cola Corporation. It's an amazing product. This little drink of carbonated sugar water is the focus of the sixth largest American public company, a company whose annual sales exceed the entire economies of many of the countries where the drink is bottled and sold. This company owns more than 45 percent of the world's carbonated drinks, selling them in 160 countries. More than 650,000 people work for this company, and estimates are that some 11,500 Cokes are consumed every second—about 1 billion servings a day![1] That's mind-boggling!

But I'm about to share with you a fact more mind-boggling than the idea of selling 11,500 soft drinks in a single second. According to researcher and author Patrick Carnes, Americans annually spend more money on pornography than the Coca-Cola Company makes in its annual sales, worldwide! As the 1990s began, pornography was earning between 7 and 10 billion dollars a year.[2]

As we consider David's downfall, please don't brush off today's pornography as a harmless part of our society. We're not talking about an occasional strip bar along the interstate of life. We're talking about an evil that snakes its way into every community in America and certainly into every church family in America. We are sleeping through a terrible attack on our relationship with God. If you're intent on searching for the heart of God, rest assured you won't find Him sharing time with a person's secret glimpses at X-rated videos or an addiction to a sexually active soap opera.

What would cause a business man, a pastor, or a respectable college student to slip into the back parking lot of a strip bar under the cover of darkness? What would cause a woman to flirt with the men in her office, hoping to take the flirting further than the married men ever dreamed of going? What would cause a father to sexually abuse his own children, or a young person to break all the rules on date after date after date?

Little steps of compromise, that's what. Looking at the wrong photographs just for a moment. Letting the eyes linger on the wrong thing for more than a moment. Justifying the action as normal or not as bad as it seems. Psychologists who deal with people who have buried themselves deep into sexual addictions tell us that without exception, all of them—all of us—have protests and excuses.

"Hey," says the man at the strip bar, "at least I've never molested children."

"Wait a minute," says the flirter at the office, "I've never been in a strip bar."

"It's just pictures," says the student looking at the pornography. "I'm not hurting anybody."

"It's because my wife doesn't meet my needs," says the man with the prostitute. "Besides, I've committed no crime."

Do you see the pattern? It's easy for each person to reserve one special sin away from view and to excuse it. "Sure," we say, "all have sinned and fall short of the glory of God, but my sin is a misdemeanor. It won't hurt me or anyone else."

If nothing's wrong, why do strip bars have parking lots out of view from the road? If nothing's wrong, why does so much lustful activity take place behind closed doors or under the cover of darkness? If nothing's wrong, why is there so much pain in the breakup of marriages, in an arrest, in the loss of a job?

You might be thinking that I'm making a mountain out of a mole hill or too big a deal out of what modern courts are calling "free speech," what Hollywood is calling "alternative lifestyles," or what our culture has often referred to as "sexual liberation." But Jesus didn't think that little steps of compromise were no big deal. He said it like this: If a man has harbored lustful thoughts in his heart, he has already committed adultery (see Matt. 5:28).

I'll tell you another reason why David pretended that what he had done hadn't hurt anyone else. Sexual sin creates a selfishness like few other sins. Perhaps that's why the Bible speaks out so strongly against this type of sin. The Bible sees the hurt that comes from rampant selfishness. The child molester doesn't stop to think of the pain, the hurt, and the tragedy that will come upon the child. The viewer of pornography doesn't stop to think that those being photographed are being taken advantage of, trapped in an endless cycle of destruction. The promiscuous spouse doesn't stop to think about the sexually transmitted diseases he or she might be bringing back to a husband or wife. The teenager on a selfish quest doesn't stop to think about the emotional and financial cost to parents that results from raising a child out of wedlock or from trying to deal with an illness like AIDS. Sexual sin, like all sin, is consumed in selfishness.

David didn't care about Bathsheba's husband, her children, her parents, her friends. David didn't care about his own family, the people he worked with, or the people who would hear about his crime. David certainly didn't care what God thought about his lust. David's heart was obsessed and driven by temptation. Satan took David down just as surely as he'll take you or me down. We have to be on our guard against these attacks.

As we move forward, remember that all the following destruction in David's life started with a simple, "harmless" look at

Bathsheba. At the time, David didn't even know the woman's name. But he did know that this woman wasn't his wife. David shouldn't have been looking. But it was a "free shot." He could rationalize it easily. No one would know. No one would care. But when he broke that one little rule, when he compromised just a little bit, the sins started clogging the arteries of David's relationship with God. The heart attack nearly killed David, and it will stand a good chance of killing you and me, too.

There is good news on the way. News that we can use to break sinful patterns, habits, and addictions. It's tough. It may be tougher than anything you face in your Christian walk, but it can be done. Before we get to that, let's see what God's Word says about sexual sin.

God's Clear Warning

God's Word clearly addresses sexual sin. Here are just three passages—there are many more—where God addresses sexual immorality:

> "Are you still so dull?" Jesus asked them. "Don't you see that whatever enters the mouth goes into the stomach and then out of the body? But the things that come out of the mouth come from the heart, and these make a man 'unclean.' For *out of the heart* come evil thoughts, murder, adultery, sexual immorality, theft, false testimony, slander. These are what make a man 'unclean'; but eating with unwashed hands does not make him 'unclean.'"
> —Matthew 15:16–20, emphasis added

If you choose to be a person after God's own heart, you'll see an immediate contrast. In God's heart, there is no sin. In our hearts, there is a root of sin that seems to stubbornly grow, always, always, always. You can pour poison on it, you can dig it up, you can burn it. But sin is the most stubborn root you'll ever find. It manages to live exactly as long as you do!

Therefore God gave them over in the sinful desires of their hearts to sexual impurity for the degrading of their bodies with one another. *They exchanged the truth of God for a lie,* and worshiped and served created things rather than the Creator—who is forever praised. Amen.

Because of this, God gave them over to shameful lusts. Even their women exchanged natural relations for un-natural ones. In the same way the men also abandoned natural relations with women and were inflamed with lust for one another. Men committed indecent acts with other men, and received in themselves the due penalty for their perversion.

—Romans 1:24–27, emphasis added

Did you see it? *Sexual sin is a lie that keeps us from the truth of God.* Think about it. God invented sex, but God gave us the gift of sex to be used within strict confines. God created nothing by accident, and when our sexuality creates pleasure inside the marriage relationship, remember that God intentionally created sex to be a pleasurable experience. Satan, the master liar, immediately says: "You want to know *real pleasure?* Come over here and experience another kind of sexual activity. God put too many rules on you, too many limitations. Look how inviting *this* is." And the heart attack warning signals light up. God gave the truth, and Satan gives the lie. Would you really want to exchange the truth of God for a lie?

Stepping past God-given boundaries always brings a penalty. You cannot have the truth of God and the lie of sexual sin at the same time. You cannot harbor both a love for sin and a love for God in your heart at the same time. It's like trying to be in New York and Los Angeles at the same time. You can't do it. You can be one place or the other, but you can't be in both places at the same time. There is no sin in the presence of God. If you harbor sin, you're pushing God right off the throne of your life. If you invite God to not only be your Savior but also Lord, ruler, and leader, that love for sin has to leave.

Once again, let me restate our first principle—Satan will constantly be about the business of attacking your spiritual heart. It's a constant, sly, and dangerous threat to your relationship with God. Harboring a sexual addiction will not get you thrown out of heaven. It will simply keep you from enjoying a full and meaningful relationship with God. It'll kill your joy. It'll steal your mind. It'll destroy all the plans God has for you. It'll remove the word "genuine" from your spiritual vocabulary.

There is also the clear, frightening warning of these words:

> The acts of the sinful nature are obvious: sexual immorality, impurity and debauchery; idolatry and witchcraft; hatred, discord, jealousy, fits of rage, selfish ambition, dissensions, factions and envy; drunkenness, orgies, and the like. I warn you, as I did before, that those who live like this will not inherit the kingdom of God.
>
> —Galatians 5:19–21

The list of Galatians 5 is amazing. The act of the sinful nature is what the Bible calls sexual immorality. Other translations might use the words "fornication," "adultery," "unchastity," "impurity," and even "sexual vice." The reason for the disparity is the broad word in the original Greek text, the word *porneia*. It is a word so broad in its definition of sexual wrongs that it eventually led to our word "pornography." The last step, the last "bookend" of Galatians' list of evils, is "orgies," a Greek word that referred to the drunken reveling of pagan feasts. It's a fifteen-step progression from *porneia*—or pornography!—to orgies, the way sin will take you further and further and further into places where you do not want to go.

The Bible says that a sinful addiction, *especially* a sexual addiction, puts you in a bad crowd, perhaps forever. Only salvation through Christ will free you. Only discipleship in following Christ will keep you free.

People who aren't saved might very well live in any of these categories. Their only hope is to find Christ, to be set free from the bondage of sin. Now here's a question: Are you saved? Have you been set free? Let me ask another question. Why would a Christian voluntarily give up living for the Lord to live with the folks who call Galatians 5:19–21 home? Would you really want to live with idolaters, witches, drunks, evildoers, and troublemakers? Many Christians trade a walk with Christ for a walk with this crowd every day. Like David, they take a peek at temptation and can't find the willpower to walk away.

It all comes back to spiritual warfare. Satan will fight you with every weapon of temptation, and you will have to make a decision to fight back. If you don't fight back, you'll get run over by a well-organized attack. It was obvious before we began that the Bible would speak out on the issue of sexual sin. But what about the help? How do we fight Satan's attacks?

God's Clear Instruction

God's Word gives us clear instructions on how to battle the sins of the heart. Listen to what the Bible says. It's as if the passage was written just for us!

Watch Out for the Darkness

> And do this, understanding the present time. The hour has come for you to wake up from your slumber, because our salvation is nearer now than when we first believed. The night is nearly over; the day is almost here. So let us put aside the *deeds of darkness* and put on the armor of light. Let us behave decently, as in the daytime, not in orgies and drunkenness, not in sexual immorality and debauchery, not in dissension and jealousy. Rather, clothe yourselves with the Lord Jesus Christ, and do not think about how to gratify the desires of the sinful nature.
>
> —Romans 13:11–14, emphasis added

This says to me that we must take action to stop all sin. Putting on the armor of God, or clothing ourselves with Jesus Christ, is a first and fundamental step. *Not thinking about* how we can satisfy our sinful nature is another obvious but often forgotten step.

Decide to Practice Discipline

"Everything is permissible for me"—but not everything is beneficial. "Everything is permissible for me"—but I will not be mastered by anything. "Food for the stomach and the stomach for food"—but God will destroy them both. The body is not meant for sexual immorality, but for the Lord, and the Lord for the body. By his power God raised the Lord from the dead, and he will raise us also. Do you not know that your bodies are members of Christ himself? Shall I then take the members of Christ and unite them with a prostitute? Never! Do you not know that he who unites himself with a prostitute is one with her in body? For it is said, "The two will become one flesh." But he who unites himself with the Lord is one with him in spirit.

—1 Corinthians 6:12–17

This is so simple. We must determine, we must decide, to practice godly discipline. Be aware that sexual sin is a very personal affront to you and to God.

If You Have to, Run!

Flee from sexual immorality. All other sins a man commits are outside his body, but he who sins sexually sins against his own body. Do you not know that your body is a temple of the Holy Spirit, who is in you, whom you have received from God? You are not your own; you were bought at a price. Therefore honor God with your body.

—1 Corinthians 6:18–20

Like Joseph running from Potipher's wife, we must sometimes literally run from sexual sin (see Gen. 39). We must leave or turn away. We must do something physically to remove ourselves from the problem. Sin is so attractive, our human desire is to take a comfortable seat and enjoy it. But when we practice spiritual discipline, when we do what's right, especially with sexual purity, we are honoring God. It is a personal form of worship. This kind of obedience is more precious to God than our attending a formal worship service.

Don't Play with Fire

> But among you there must not be even a hint of sexual immorality, or of any kind of impurity, or of greed, because these are improper for God's holy people. Nor should there be obscenity, foolish talk or coarse joking, which are out of place, but rather thanksgiving. For of this you can be sure: No immoral, impure or greedy person—such a man is an idolater—has any inheritance in the kingdom of Christ and of God. Let no one deceive you with empty words, for because of such things God's wrath comes on those who are disobedient. Therefore do not be partners with them.
>
> —Ephesians 5:3–7

It's a simple principle: Don't play with the smallest bit of fire. David looked once, and then looked again. It cost him dearly. You and I must do this simple thing: Draw the line at the first sign of trouble and do not cross that line.

Do Whatever It Takes

> Put to death, therefore, whatever belongs to your earthly nature: sexual immorality, impurity, lust, evil desires and greed, which is idolatry. Because of these, the wrath of God is coming.
>
> —Colossians 3:5–6

Wherever Satan is attacking your heart, do whatever it takes to kill that sinful practice. Remove the television or the video player. Take a different route home from work. Change jobs. Fall to your knees and pray, right in the midst of temptation, wherever you are. I tell you the truth: You cannot fall on your knees and pray and continue to sin at the same time. What you must do here is simple: Do whatever it takes to end sinful practices.

You Can Learn Control!

> It is God's will that you should be sanctified: that you should avoid sexual immorality; that each of you should learn to control his own body in a way that is holy and honorable, not in passionate lust like the heathen, who do not know God; and that in this matter no one should wrong his brother or take advantage of him. The Lord will punish men for all such sins, as we have already told you and warned you. For God did not call us to be impure, but to live a holy life. Therefore, he who rejects this instruction does not reject man but God, who gives you his Holy Spirit.
>
> —1 Thessalonians 4:3–8

You can learn to control your body and any sinful addiction. Learning, however, takes time. Don't be discouraged at early failure. Simply determine to learn, to make progress.

Almost certainly, someone reading these words is frowning. There certainly is disagreement in our culture about what is right and wrong concerning sexuality. But hear me out. The Bible is so incredibly clear on these points that it's impossible to get this wrong. How else could God make it any clearer?

It is not easy to accept difficult teaching. These instructions, however, are amazingly simple. And the Bible says that whoever "rejects this instruction does not reject man, but God, who gives you his Holy Spirit." Listen to the Holy Spirit, who confirms: "Yes, this is true."

Satan the Tempter

There is more to the story of David and Bathsheba, much more, and we'll cover more of it in the next chapter. For now, remember this: The temptation that nearly destroyed these two people will certainly come after you. Don't forget who you're dealing with!

From my files of illustrations comes a story that's a perfect way to wrap this up. It's the story of Major William Martin, a British subject who is buried near Huelvo on the southern coast of Spain. Martin never knew the great contribution he made to the Allied success in the Second World War, especially in Sicily. Before he ever saw the battle front, he died of pneumonia in the foggy dampness of England.

The Allies had invaded North Africa. The next logical step was Sicily. Knowing the Germans calculated this, the Allies determined to outfox them. One dark night, an Allied submarine came to the surface just off the coast of Spain and put Martin's body out to sea in a rubber raft with an oar. In his pocket were "secret documents" indicating the Allied forces would strike next in Greece and Sardinia.

Major Martin's body washed ashore, and Axis intelligence operatives soon found him, thinking he had crashed at sea. They passed the phony documents through Axis hands all the way to Hitler's headquarters. While Allied forces moved toward Sicily, thousands and thousands of German troops moved on to Greece and Sardinia—where the battle wasn't.

Satan is a lot more cunning than that, and one of his favorite areas to attack is in the area of sexual temptation. It's possible even as you've read these words that the Liar has whispered, "Don't worry about sexual temptation. That could *never* happen to you."

It happened to David, a man who had been given the lofty title of a man after God's own heart. It has happened to countless millions of people who felt it would never happen to them. After all, all they had ever really done was commit a few "misdemeanor" sins.

David's heart attack left him writhing in pain, and his story is a warning for all of us. Do whatever it takes, David seems to be telling us, to not let it happen to us.

CHAPTER 14

Recovering from a "Heart Attack"

The day started with such promise. He had always wanted a red Porsche, and on October 17, 1989, a man by the name of Jones finally got what he wanted. It was loaded, it was red, and it was his.

On top of the excitement of buying a new sports car, our Mr. Jones also had tickets to the World Series! He drove the Porsche to Candlestick Park in San Francisco, found his way into the stadium, took a seat, and watched the day turn sour.

First, there was the earthquake. Perhaps you remember the nationally televised shaking that postponed the game and paralyzed the San Francisco and Oakland areas. For Mr. Jones, it meant fear and the loss of a perfect evening.

In the parking lot, things got worse. He discovered that his brand new car was stolen! It was several days before police identified the missing car, crushed and useless underneath the collapsed Nimitz Freeway.

What a bad day. No game, an earthquake, and a stolen, crushed car. It wasn't fair!

The thief, however, had an even worse day. He was driving the red dream when the earthquake struck, and when the freeway fell, he died in the very instrument of his wrongdoing.

For centuries, the Bible has warned that our sins will find us out. Eventually, even in modern America, we can all see that sin carries a terrible price. It'll leave you dead in a pile of rubble bigger than you've ever imagined.

Let's think about recovering from heart attacks. Surviving a heart attack is a tough thing to do. Heart attack victims whom I've been around suddenly tend to hate the foods, the fats, and the stress of the years that caused them so much pain and so much time in a hospital room they never planned to visit. They have a tough time adjusting to a new diet, a new exercise plan, and certainly, a new sense of vulnerability. It's a tough road back to good health.

This stage of David's life underscores the costly nature of sin and the after-effects of a sin buildup in the arteries of one's relationship with God. The lifestyle of King David was one that guaranteed a spiritual heart attack.

By the time he hears that Bathsheba is pregnant, David has no intention of being responsible for his sin. Uriah, Bathsheba's husband, won't cooperate with David's scheme, so the king arranges for his soldier to die. Adultery. Murder. Lies. An intentional drawing back from the presence of God. David seems to be oblivious to the chest pains signaling a great attack on his spiritual heart.

We pick up the story at the end of 2 Samuel 11.

> When Uriah's wife heard that her husband was dead, she mourned for him. After the time of mourning was over, David had her brought to his house, and she became his wife and bore him a son. But the thing David had done displeased the LORD.
>
> —vv. 26–27

We read these verses quickly, and as we make the transition into chapter 12, perhaps we forget that much time has passed. Several months go by in the kingdom, perhaps a year or more. It's not just another year. This is a year of nonrepentance. A year of living a lie. A year of blowing off a lifetime of walking with God. A year when David believes he's gotten away with murder.

But though God is slow to anger, God does get angry. The earthquake is starting to rumble. God picks a preacher named Nathan to communicate with His unrepentant king. Nathan gets David's attention through a story. David believes the story to be true. In reality, the story is a parable. In reality, the story is a trap set for a king. In reality, the encounter is that moment when David clutches his chest and finally feels the pain of his spiritual heart attack. It's a moment when David will either live with God or die without the Lord. The days that follow will be, as a doctor would say, critical. Every movement is watched, for the patient is at the weakest point of his spiritual life.

> The LORD sent Nathan to David. When he came to him, he said, "There were two men in a certain town, one rich and the other poor. The rich man had a very large number of sheep and cattle, but the poor man had nothing except one little ewe lamb he had bought. He raised it, and it grew up with him and his children. It shared his food, drank from his cup and even slept in his arms. It was like a daughter to him.
>
> "Now a traveler came to the rich man, but the rich man refrained from taking one of his own sheep or cattle to prepare a meal for the traveler who had come to him. Instead, he took the ewe lamb that belonged to the poor man and prepared it for the one who had come to him."
>
> David burned with anger against the man and said to Nathan, "As surely as the LORD lives, the man who did this deserves to die! He must pay for that lamb four times over, because he did such a thing and had no pity."

Then Nathan said to David, "You are the man! This is what the LORD, the God of Israel, says: 'I anointed you king over Israel, and I delivered you from the hand of Saul. I gave your master's house to you, and your master's wives into your arms. I gave you the house of Israel and Judah. And if all this had been too little, I would have given you even more. Why did you despise the word of the LORD by doing what is evil in his eyes? You struck down Uriah the Hittite with the sword and took his wife to be your own. You killed him with the sword of the Ammonites. Now, therefore, the sword will never depart from your house, because you despised me and took the wife of Uriah the Hittite to be your own.'

"This is what the LORD says: 'Out of your own household I am going to bring calamity upon you. Before your very eyes I will take your wives and give them to one who is close to you, and he will lie with your wives in broad daylight. You did it in secret, but I will do this thing in broad daylight before all Israel.'"

Then David said to Nathan, "I have sinned against the LORD."

Nathan replied, "The LORD has taken away your sin. You are not going to die. But because by doing this you have made the enemies of the LORD show utter contempt, the son born to you will die."

After Nathan had gone home, the LORD struck the child that Uriah's wife had borne to David, and he became ill. David pleaded with God for the child. He fasted and went into his house and spent the nights lying on the ground. The elders of his household stood beside him to get him up from the ground, but he refused, and he would not eat any food with them.

On the seventh day the child died. David's servants were afraid to tell him that the child was dead, for they thought, "While the child was still living, we spoke to

David but he would not listen to us. How can we tell him the child is dead? He may do something desperate."

David noticed that his servants were whispering among themselves and he realized the child was dead. "Is the child dead?" he asked.

"Yes," they replied, "he is dead."

Then David got up from the ground. After he had washed, put on lotions and changed his clothes, he went into the house of the LORD and worshiped. Then he went to his own house, and at his request they served him food, and he ate.

His servants asked him, "Why are you acting this way? While the child was alive, you fasted and wept, but now that the child is dead, you get up and eat!"

He answered, "While the child was still alive, I fasted and wept. I thought, 'Who knows? The LORD may be gracious to me and let the child live.' But now that he is dead, why should I fast? Can I bring him back again? I will go to him, but he will not return to me."

Then David comforted his wife Bathsheba, and he went to her and lay with her. She gave birth to a son, and they named him Solomon. The LORD loved him; and because the LORD loved him, he sent word through Nathan the prophet to name him Jedidiah.

—2 Samuel 12:1–25

In the last chapter, we covered the principles that got David into this mess. For starters, if you're going to be a person who seeks after God's own heart, you must expect to see spiritual attacks, what I'm calling Satan's "heart attacks." He's going after your spiritual heart, and he's going to use temptation as his main weapon. I'm convinced that pornography is one of Satan's favorite tools, his potent poison for the heart. To do as David did, to take a glance and then to return for the drinking in of the lust, is to drink in one of the worst poisons you could ever bring upon your heart. We can't search for God with our hearts and stand at the same time with David on the rooftop. David played with temptation, and David lost his walk with God. You and I are no different.

Two other things we've already covered are the plain-talking way the Bible speaks to sexual sin and the help Scripture has for us to prevent heart attacks. Here's another critical help that Scripture gives us: A spiritual heart attack cannot be survived without repentance.

Repentance Must Lead

In our search for God's heart, repentance must lead the way. We move past the coals of the fire, past the flickering flames, past the yellow and red flames of the fire's energy, and finally, we reach the white-hot center of the fire. Right here. Right now.

If you have anything in you that desires to be a person after God's own heart, put yourself in the Scripture as if you were there. Imagine you were there. Watch it with me.

David is holding court again. He's on his throne, and nothing is denied him. There is a table of the richest food nearby. Scantily dressed concubines mill about in the foyer. Perhaps a wife is there. If not one wife, there are six others nearby, waiting on David's beck and call. If the girls in the harem or his first seven wives don't satisfy David's sexual appetite, there is Bathsheba, the newcomer. As for her part, Bathsheba has dealt with her grief by enjoying the lavish spending habits of the king, her new husband. She mourns, surely, for her dead Uriah and for the purity she had felt before the one-night fling. David has done his best to make her feel good. He is her escape. Her pregnancy had been something of an embarrassment, but the king made her feel that everything was OK. The baby was his, and the world knew it, and there seemed to be no shame in what they had done. David had, in fact, led a year-long national revolution that removed shame from sin.

His throne room is a busy and important place. Perhaps, on one side of the room, the men of war boast of their victories. In another corner, important men discuss the kingdom's finances. The treasury is full, and the economy is bursting. Another group of men surround the king himself. They tell the king stories, listen to his tales, and laugh at the king's jokes. He is in charge of the kingdom, and the kingdom looks great. To look at this scene is to realize very quickly that there is absolutely nothing this powerful, commanding, popular man cannot have if he sets his heart on it.

You might note that amid the flowers, the rich curtains, the gold ornaments, and the palace music, there is no Scripture. There are no Levites singing praises to God. David's harp is holding a dusty place on the wall in a backroom storage closet. The songs of praise to God are sung by a few professional priests, not by David, in another building out of earshot. David's attendance at the tabernacle has noticeably changed since his walk on the rooftop several months before. The king, it seems, doesn't take joy in being around God's people these days. When he's in a worship service, his mind seems to be somewhere else.

For months, perhaps a year, David has forgotten God. The boy who had taken down a giant enemy with only a slingshot and a prayer was far, far removed from this man who now had enough money to make it in life without God. This man had tasted sin, and he decided to drink the whole, delicious cup. He got drunk on the wine of sexual addiction, of never saying no to his physical desires, and the wine turned out to be poison for his soul.

By looking at the scene, however, you'd never know the man had been drinking poison. You'd never know the king was about to experience chest-wrenching pain that would throw him headfirst into the greatest agony of his life. No, the king's palace looked lavish, spectacular, and incredibly rich. The king looked secure, confident, and untouchable.

Certainly, the prophet must have looked out of place. Nathan came into the room, without a name-brand stitch of clothing on his body. He looked mighty plain, sort of torn and ragged. But his bony shoulders stood straight, and his thin face held steely eyes. He needed to talk to the king. No doubt, Nathan was frightened.

His heart was in his throat. Did he really want this assignment from God, this suicide mission from heaven? The king would not take kindly to a rebuke. Nathan knew this day might very well be his last day on earth.

Somewhere in the fasting of the week before, God had given the prophet a story. "There's a problem in the village," started the prophet, and David was hooked.

"Tell me. I'll solve the problem," says the king.

Nathan quilts the story, piece by piece, and the king's court is covered in the trap. They all stop to listen. A poor man with a poor family has just one sheep, Nathan says. A little lamb, really, and it's a family pet. It eats at their table, even. A rich man, the next-door neighbor, has plenty of sheep and cattle and rams and goats. He has money galore. He has it all. But when the visitors came, he stole the poor family's one and only lamb and killed it. They ate on it, feasted on it, and showed no shame.

The lamb even might have been the one reserved for Passover. If the family took its relationship with God very seriously, it would have taken this passover lamb into its family circle for the better part of a year. It would be greatly loved by this family, by the children, so that the family would feel great pain when the lamb was slain for their sins a year later.

As Nathan tells the story, every heart is pierced with the wrong that had been done to this simple family, this family trying to be right before God. Why, this was a sacred offense! This lamb was something that belonged to God, and to God alone. This lamb was as sacred before God as, well, *marriage*.

And another man had stolen this sacred possession. King David is enraged. He has no clue of the trap that has been set.

"That man deserves to die!" roars the king. Everyone in the palace agrees, and shouts of approval resound. Remember this, as David continues to talk: David is so powerful, his word is the law. If the king makes a decision, there is no higher court to reverse the judgment.

David talks, passing judgment on himself. "He deserves to die, but here's what he shall do," says the king. "He shall repay his wrongdoing fourfold. He stole one life, let him give four lives for it." The king's court nods its approval, ready to congratulate the king for his wisdom. But then silence covers the room. Something quite unexpected is happening.

The bony finger of Nathan the prophet is slicing, slicing through the air, and now is pointing right at the most powerful man in all the world. All the music stops. The concubines had found reason to listen in, and they are dumbfounded. The men of war are frozen. The clinking of the money-counting is silenced. All eyes are on the drama in the throne room. Bathsheba turns to see the finger pointed at her new husband.

"King David . . . *you* . . . are . . . the . . . man!"

Now here it is! It's the moment of truth. It's the moment when nothing else matters. David will either be a man after God's own heart, or he will go the pitiful, tragic way of Saul. It's the moment in the operating room when, spiritually, David flat-lines. The only hope of restarting this very sick heart is the shock of repentance. Bold, cold, full-powered repentance.

And the victory in the midst of tragedy comes in verse 13: "Then David said to Nathan, 'I have sinned against the LORD.'"

It was a heartbroken repentance. It was an "I-take-all-the-blame" repentance. It was an "I'll-change-my-lifestyle" repentance. The heart monitor has a few weak blips coming back. David is barely alive, but he is alive. In a few shaken moments, David is struggling to make it to the tabernacle. He calls for the dusty harp, and he starts to sing before the Lord. How fortunate we are that the first words of Psalm 51 tell us the circumstances of the song. The song, the Bible tells us, is the one David composed after Nathan had confronted him.

Listen to portions of the song; listen to the heart of a repentant man.

> Have mercy on me, O God,
>   according to your unfailing love;
> according to your great compassion
>   blot out my transgressions.

Wash away all my iniquity
   and cleanse me from my sin.

For I know my transgressions,
   and my sin is always before me.
Against you, you only, have I sinned
   and done what is evil in your sight,
so that you are proved right when you speak
   and justified when you judge.

—vv. 1–4

Surely you desire truth in the inner parts. . . .

   Cleanse me with hyssop, and I will be clean;
   wash me, and I will be whiter than snow.

—vv. 6–7

Hide your face from my sins
   and blot out all my iniquity.

Create in me a pure heart, O God,
   and renew a steadfast spirit within me.
Do not cast me from your presence
   or take your Holy Spirit from me.
Restore to me the joy of your salvation
   and grant me a willing spirit, to sustain me.

—vv. 9–12

David's walk with God was eventually restored. Eventually, in time, he was able to walk in victory again. In time, he was able to feel washed completely clean of his sin. In time, he would feel freed from the shackles of what his version of pornography had started. In time, his heart would beat strongly again.

But do not skim quickly over this truth: None of the victory would have come if there hadn't been this critical, crucial moment of repentance—none of it.

The same is still true. If your heart has been poisoned with sin, you will not find the cure without repentance. God's Word is plainly, painfully, explicitly clear. We must face our sin squarely in the face, admit that the sin is ours and ours alone, and ask God to forgive us. There are no exceptions. Not for a powerful king in a rich throne room, not for anyone reading these words.

Consequences Always Follow

Forgiveness washes away the spiritual wrong, but sin always carries its consequences. People who have been through physical heart attacks and those who have had bypass surgery know that life is never the same after the heart attack, or even after the near attack. You can survive, and you can live a healthy life again, but life will never be the same.

Things change. Maybe there is no salt on your table. Maybe there is a new diet of low-fat foods. Maybe there is a new list of forbidden fruits on your dining-room table. Maybe there is an exercise regime. Maybe there is early retirement. A physical heart attack changes the rest of your life.

So does a spiritual heart attack. If you don't prevent it, expect to pay a big price for playing with poison. An old preacher once said: "Sin will always take you farther than you wanted to go, keep you longer than you planned to stay, and cost you more than you wanted to pay."

Know this: David was immediately forgiven in God's eyes, but his life was never the same—never. The things that happened in David's life in the wake of his sin with Bathsheba were devastating. Bathsheba's child, the one conceived by David's lust, was already born. Already grabbing the hearts of his parents. The child was already smiling, sleeping, cuddling with its mother. The child became ill. David fasted, prayed, begged God for another chance. But the baby died.

Then there was Tamar, David's daughter. She was a teenager, looking forward to a great marriage somewhere down the road. There would be, somewhere, somehow, a great life. But her brother

Amnon, imitating his father's "never-say-no" attitude to his lust, became infatuated with his sister's physical beauty. In short, he raped her, his own sister. Immediately, Amnon hated his sister. Tamar was heartbroken, and her dreams for marriage and for a beautiful life were over. Though she lived, there were many ways in which her life was gone. The joy, the sparkle of her eyes, was crushed and dulled.

Absalom waited two years for his father to punish Amnon. When there was no action, Absalom acted. He murdered his brother. In a short period of time, Absalom's taste for blood-letting and for power increased. He rebelled against his father, slept with his father's concubines in full view of the city, and then took over the kingdom. The revolt was short-lived. Absalom was killed.

David's one night of lustful sin, his one year of living a lie, was taking a terrible toll. Think of it. The baby. Tamar. Amnon. Absalom.

One. Two. Three. Four.

Do you remember David's words to Nathan the prophet? "That man deserves to die. But he shall repay fourfold."

Now we've got to be careful here. Does God kill our children because of our sin? No! If God killed our children because of our sin, none of our children would be alive and neither would we!

No, God doesn't kill our children. But there are times when we kill them—in a way—because of our sin. Commit adultery, and divorce may split your home wide open. The innocence of childhood dies for your children, and it dies quickly. The pain is always remembered. Commit murder, and children do without the imprisoned parent. Absence is absence, whether you're in prison or in a grave or in a different home from your spouse.

This story is not saying that if we commit sexual sin, God will kill our children. What this incredible Bible story does for us is illustrate in a very, very vivid way that while sin may be forgiven by God, the consequences of our sin may be carried on for years and years and years.

Please remember this: For David, all this destruction started with a simple look at a naked woman who was not his wife. It was

David's version of what we call pornography. The message of today is clear. Draw some lines of protection around your heart.
Fight the heart attack before it happens. Don't let Satan laugh in
your face because of his sly, crafty attacks.

God's Grace Forgives

God's grace is abundantly able to forgive even the worst of our
sins. It's time for some great, great words of hope.

I spent some time recently looking through the Gospels at the
words of Jesus, looking for condemnation of this man, David,
who committed murder, adultery, and cover-up. I spent time looking for the way Jesus would blister David's dysfunctional parenting
skills, the way he blew it time after time after time.

Do you know what I found? Not one word of condemnation.
Instead, I found angels, John the Baptist, and others pointing to
the place of Jesus' birth and to the great city of Jerusalem and
calling both the "City of David." It's a point of honor for both
Bethlehem, the king's birthplace, and for Jerusalem. In the Gospels, Jesus is called, over and over again, the "Son of David." Jesus
used David as a positive example at least twice. Reading the New
Testament, you'd get the idea that Jesus, the Son of God, witness
of history, witness of all sin, somehow couldn't even remember
David's sin.

That, my friend, is exactly the point. We will live with the consequences of our sin for an entire lifetime. I promise. We know it,
and we remember it. We can't forget it. But when God forgives,
God also forgets. When we go through the painful process of
repentance, the fire that burns across our hearts purifies us. God
washes away the sin, never more to bring it up.

That's amazing. That's grace so amazing, as writer Philip Yancey
said so well, it's not amazing at all. It's scandalous.

David was able, in time, to restore the integrity to his life. He,
in time, had a right relationship with his wife, with his children,
with his kingdom. He was able to give sound advice to Solomon,
who would become the wisest man the world had ever known.

God's grace was able to cover every mistake David had ever made. God's grace will cover your mistakes, too. It may take a while before you feel the freedom from the shackles sin has placed upon you. But you know what? It took a while for you to get into trouble, too. There may be consequences to your sin that live on even after God forgives you. But if you don't repent with David, you'll die with Saul. It may be a painful experience to fall to your knees and say: "I have sinned against the Lord." But how much more painful it is to ignore sin, to pay a greater price, and to lose your life, even as you live.

Just One Little Bite

Perhaps you have heard about the little fly that has caused so much trouble in Africa. You'll find the fly along Africa's fastest-flowing rivers. Once this tiny, tiny fly bites someone, it begins to breed in the human body. It begins its life as an almost microscopic dot—something so small, no one would seem to notice for more than a moment. But before you know it, it has produced thousands of worms that migrate throughout the body, even settling in the eyes where, believe it or not, one worm can grow up to thirty inches long. The disease *(onchocersiasis)* is commonly called "River Blindness," and right now, it is depriving millions of their sight as well as disfiguring an estimated fifteen million people in sixteen different African nations.

In two chapters, we have covered a lot of ground. We have looked at the massive devastation caused by David's flirtation with just a little bit of sin. He was a man after God's own heart, but Satan kept throwing "heart attacks" at the king.

And finally, there was a bite. Finally, there was an area where David figured it was safe to take a break from godliness. He'd just take a harmless look at a nameless woman. After all, what could happen? Who would object? And one little sin led to thoughts, the thoughts led to action, the action led to lies, the lies led to a cover-up, and it all led to spiritual blindness. It all led to disaster. Sin took David farther than he wanted to go, cost him more than he wanted to pay, and created more havoc than he had ever imagined.

The key to avoiding the danger, to surviving the heart attack, is to prevent the attack in the first place. Draw the line. Don't cross the line. Spot the danger zones, and don't go there. Stop the relationship that has even the slightest hint of wrongdoing. Pray to God in heaven that He'll give you protection, courage, wisdom, and integrity.

Perhaps you're well along in the recovery process. I would like to encourage you to bathe in God's forgiveness and move on with your life. David and Bathsheba must have been heartbroken, absolutely heartbroken, after their sin was exposed. He must have kicked himself a thousand times as he saw lonely Tamar or went past the graves of Amnon and Absalom. She must have longed for Uriah. Both of them longed to hold their infant child. Their mistakes were ever before them. But they had to move on.

And God helped them. Bathsheba recovered well enough to be the mother of Solomon, the next king. David recovered enough to lead, again, with integrity. He would once again become a man of great faith, a man searching for God's own heart. He made it. She made it. And so can you.

CHAPTER 15

The Last Years of the Search

As I wrote these words, I marked another birthday. And for the first time in my life, parts of my body were aching for no good reason—just hurting. The mirror says my hair is graying, and to tell you the truth, my memory is slipping. Maybe that will be OK, one day. Like one comedian said, "If I keep wandering through my house looking for the things I wanted to find just one room ago, it won't be long, at this rate, before I can hide my own Easter eggs. I'll just hide them, leave the room for a moment, and then return, having a great time finding the surprises!"

Did you read what the one-hundred-two-year-old woman said when they asked her about the benefits of living to age 102? She paused, then said, "Well, there's no peer pressure!"

Another old-timer was having fun at a senior citizen's seminar when a young woman asked him what kind of plans he had for the future. The seventy-five-year-old man said, "Honey, at my age, I don't even buy green bananas."

But one of the worst stories I've heard is of the grandchild sitting on her granddaddy's lap listening to the Bible story of

Noah's Ark. "Were you in the ark, Grandpa?" The older man chuckled and answered, "Why, no I wasn't." There was a pause, and the child looked at him quizzically and asked, "Then why weren't you drowned?"

Time moves on! And what if most of your time has moved on? What if you're already past your prime time? Does the Bible have anything to say to a person in retirement or to a person who has simply admitted that he's not as young as he used to be?

Sure! The answer is simple. If you're past your prime time, keep searching for God's own heart and never stop. Make sure your last years of the search for God's own heart are your best years. Our biblical example comes late in the life of David, as found in 2 Samuel.

> Once again there was a battle between the Philistines and Israel. David went down with his men to fight against the Philistines, and he became exhausted. And Ishbi-Benob, one of the descendants of Rapha, whose bronze spearhead weighed three hundred shekels and who was armed with a new sword, said he would kill David. But Abishai son of Zeruiah came to David's rescue; he struck the Philistine down and killed him. Then David's men swore to him, saying, "Never again will you go out with us to battle, so that the lamp of Israel will not be extinguished."
>
> In the course of time, there was another battle with the Philistines, at Gob. At that time Sibbecai the Hushathite killed Saph, one of the descendants of Rapha.
>
> In another battle with the Philistines at Gob, Elhanan son of Jaare-Oregim the Bethlehemite killed Goliath the Gittite, who had a spear with a shaft like a weaver's rod.
>
> In still another battle, which took place at Gath, there was a huge man with six fingers on each hand and six toes on each foot—twenty-four in all. He also was de-

scended from Rapha. When he taunted Israel, Jonathan son of Shimeah, David's brother, killed him.

These four were descendants of Rapha in Gath, and they fell at the hands of David and his men.

—2 Samuel 21:15–22

The Exhausting Passage of Time

Let's be honest. In time, time will exhaust you. Growing old is no picnic. You've probably heard the cracks written by folks who've seen the cracks in their faces and felt the cracks in their backs.

- "You know you are getting older when you try to straighten out the wrinkles in your socks only to find you aren't wearing any."
- "At twenty we don't care what the world thinks of us; at thirty we start to worry about what the world thinks of us; at forty we realize the world isn't thinking of us at all."
- "Forty is when you stop patting yourself on the back and start patting yourself under the chin."

George Burns, an expert on growing older, said you know you're getting older when:

- the gleam in your eye is from the sun hitting your bifocals.
- your "little black book" contains only names ending in "M.D."
- you get winded playing chess.
- your children start to look middle-aged.
- you sit in a rocking chair, but you can't get it going.
- your knees buckle, but your belt won't.
- dialing long distance wears you out.
- you burn the midnight oil at 9 P.M.
- the little gray-haired woman you help across the street is your wife.
- an attractive member of the opposite sex goes by, and your pacemaker makes the garage door go up!

- And my favorite: "You know you're getting old when you stoop to tie your shoes and wonder what else you can do while you're down there."

It's exhausting to grow older! The Bible gives us a great picture of David, in a tough moment of his life, when he realizes that time has exhausted him. No funny jokes, no comedian's routines can take away the truth: The older we get, the tougher it is to keep the battle lines strong.

Right when you're supposed to be enjoying retirement, a child goes through a divorce and returns to your home with her kids. Right when life is supposed to be slow and easy, an assignment comes that creates the greatest workload you've ever known. Right when you were planning on a leisurely vacation, an illness arrives and saps your strength and your finances. After you've given decades to your church, you look around and become frightened to see how young, and how inexperienced, the new leaders appear to be. The worry will keep you up at night. Growing older can be exhausting. That's just a fact.

I like the idea that David, after all of his failures—and he had experienced some whoppers—was out there fighting. He was going after it one more time. David wasn't going to quit. But time had taken its toll, and his men, the younger ones, saw it was very, very dangerous for David to be involved in the battle. And make no mistake about it, it was a battle. And it still is. It's an exhausting battle.

A New Generation of Problems

As you near the end of your life, you'll see a new generation of problems. Evil never takes a generation off! At the beginning of his career, David battled one giant, a big one who had paralyzed all Israel. Goliath was a huge problem, one he never forgot. But near the end of his life, not one, but four more giants came out of the woods. It overwhelmed him to see that there were still giants, problems, evil. But again, evil never takes a generation off. It seems, in fact, that things get worse and worse with each passing generation.

If you've lived a long life, you've already seen an incredible increase in evil. We have seen school-aged children shooting children and teachers. As I worked today, the local headlines told of two teenagers who apparently robbed a home and shot three members of a family, leaving a mother, a wife, to come home to a tragedy that should never have happened. She lost her entire family in a single day, a single act of horror. The captured suspects can't tell authorities exactly why they decided to start shooting. And the real horror is that this story is only *today's* story. Tomorrow will have another nightmare.

We have unparalleled filth on television and in our communities. We have seen the multiplication of alcoholic addictions, the rise of drug abuse, and political corruption like no other century before it. We have watched things come out of the closet that should be nailed shut in the darkness, and we have seen human life—from the very beginning to the very end—become less and less valuable. We have seen the phrases "child abuse," "spouse abuse," and "elder abuse" become household words.

We have seen America in church, out of church, and then back in a church that is so weak, so mild-mannered, so nonrelevant, it's hard to even recognize the product.

It'll exhaust you, but every generation has learned the same truth—evil never stops. New giants come out of the woods. New problems develop, and they look, frankly, overwhelming. I wonder if David looked up and felt terrified. Some of those giants made Goliath look like a large toddler. These giants were bigger, they had more fingers and toes, they had larger spears, they shouted louder, they were new and improved versions of the evil he had battled all his life.

Sound familiar? Don't stop with the bad news.

A New Generation of Leaders

God gives each generation the opportunity to raise up new leaders for God's people. Read the passage again. With new leaders, every one of the new giants was defeated, falling just as hard as old Goliath had fallen years before. Giants are no problem for God, as long as God has some leaders to call upon.

As David faced his last days, exhausted at the task before this new generation, the Bible records story after story of faithful men and women who answered the call to be godly leaders for their people. Turn the pages to the next of the Bible's stories, and you'll see another generation of godly leaders developed. Go through every book of the Bible, and you'll see the heroes. From Esther to Nehemiah, from Jeremiah to Daniel, God was never without someone to fight the battle.

Eventually, God Himself would join the battle and mark the victory with the cross. Don't lose your vision on God's plan, on God's faithfulness.

God will never be without a witness—I promise. An older Elijah once thought he was the last man standing for God, but God quickly told him that He had seven thousand godly people left in Israel (see 1 Kings 19:14–18). Elijah was discouraged, but God had His witnesses! When the exile came, Ezra was heartbroken, but there was still a remnant. All the way through Revelation, God always—always!—has His witnesses.

And since it's not a question that God will have witnesses in each generation, there really is only one question left—will you have a hand in raising up the leaders of the next generation?

Here are a few practical steps that might help:

1. *Look around at the "mighty men" of the next generation.* David saw four such men in chapter 21. By the end of chapter 23, the Bible says David saw thirty-seven mighty men. There were more than he realized! God has already placed around you some great young men and women, some great teenagers, who have hearts that search for God's own heart. God is, right now, preparing some other young men and women in other parts of the world who will have an important hand in leading His church. God is faithful. Looking around to see what He's already done will be a great blessing to all of us. Be encouraged, today, by the *crowd* of godly leaders already in place for the next generation!

2. *Leave your story to the next generation.* Write it down. Make

videos. Set up monuments. You've already done these kinds of things. You've built church buildings, so your grandchildren will see the grandeur of God in the architecture of the places you have helped erect to His glory. Some of you have been very visible in front of your children and grandchildren in taking care of church grounds, church property, singing in choirs, and teaching Sunday school classes. Over time, the next generation will clearly see what you decided was most important in your life. They'll be looking at decisions you're making today.

3. *Mentor a younger leader.* Pick out someone and be an encourager to that young man or woman. Brag on him or her. Establish a relationship with that person. Be a Paul to a Timothy. Be a Lydia to a young woman in the community. In time, that support from an older Christian will be like a powerful wind in the sails of that person's life. Young people need others to believe in them. You be that encourager!

I say it again: It's no question that God will raise up a new generation of leaders. The only question is this one: Will you be a part of raising up those leaders?

An older person wrote these haunting, anonymous words.

> First I was dying to finish high school and start college.
> And then I was dying to finish college and start working.
> And then I was dying for my children to grow old enough
> for school, so I could return to work.
> And then I was dying to retire.
> And now, I am dying . . . and suddenly I realize I forgot
> to live.

You know, those don't have to be your words. You can make any change you need to make, today, at any age you happen to be. You don't have to concentrate on growing older, on what you can do less, or how exhausting it all is. Just live.

CHAPTER 16

Finding the Song of Your Heart

Some years back, when I was self-absorbed in my own career and wondering how I'd ever manage to own things like a three-bedroom home in the suburbs and a car with working air-conditioning, a wonderful thing happened. I spent a week of vacation working with my father.

He was building a home in a neighboring community, taking three years to lay hammer to nail, secure PVC pipes to toilets, and lay kitchen tile. He was building his dream home in his spare time, playing carpenter while other men around him were playing golf. On this particular week, it was time to work on the roof.

From Monday through Friday, my dad and I hammered, sawed, painted, and held on to shaky scaffolding. It was a week of faith-building, for I never have been fond of heights.

To tell you the truth, it had been a very long time since I had spent time with my father. But for a solid week, we worked, ate banana sandwiches for lunch, and devoured bags of Mom's homemade cookies during afternoon breaks. In between sunrise and sunset, we talked. Sometimes we talked about shingles, sometimes we talked about life.

Something very strange happened when it came time to leave on Friday afternoon. It took only a few minutes to reach the interstate highway from my dad's house, but by the time I turned the car onto the entrance ramp, something inside me turned on the tears. It was unplanned, this burst of emotions, and I really didn't know how to handle it. Only now, with a decade and a half of time behind me, can I put into words what words will never adequately describe.

It was so simple. I had enjoyed being with my father, and I felt love for him. I missed the years that had gone by, the years when I had neglected our relationship. I suppose, near the end of my life, if I have the opportunity to reflect on the different chapters of my days, I shall look upon that one week as one of the best weeks of my life.

It was kind of funny. For years, I had been seeking the spotlight, the praise of the crowd, and the right corporate ladder to climb, thinking that one of these things would be the one thing that would make me happy. But in that wonderful week on the rooftop, there was none of the public applause I had been seeking and no promotions to be gained. There was nothing on the roof of that house except shingles, sunshine, and my dad.

By the end of the week, it all caught up with me. I was overcome with emotion, happy with this wonderful, simple discovery that I loved my father, and that he had loved me all my life.

And the lesson I close with is just as simple: Your heavenly Father loves you.

The Love of the Father

People searching for a relationship with God have been making this discovery of God's love for centuries. David learned it, even after his long list of mistakes had been written in the pages of Samuel's history.

Late in his life, David had an opportunity to be overwhelmed again by his love for the Father and the Father's love for him. The circumstances of David's rediscovery came in the midst of stress. For you see, just before his life would be over, the old king had to survive one more series of challenges.

Absalom's revolt had set all kinds of problems in motion. David had to muster his courage and his troops and retake Jerusalem. Israel and Judah were already sowing the seeds of civil war, and there were some expensive battles to wage. David fought them. And when an old enemy saw a weakened nation under David's care, the Philistines appeared again and forced four smaller, exhausting battles. David's men won all the battles, and in time, Jerusalem, all Israel, and David's reign was secure again.

For David, maybe it was like a Friday afternoon drive home when suddenly the emotion welled up inside of him and poured out in a song. Maybe there were tears, maybe there weren't. Certainly, though, there was joy in the discovery that God loved him.

The old man picked up his harp and wrote a new song, a song of his heart. Listen to the words, for there is a youthful passion in his song, a sense of a preschooler's amazement in the hand of God. In the beginning, in the middle, and at the end of this song is the overwhelming reality of God's great love. The words are recorded for us in 2 Samuel 22. As the music begins, listen first to the names of David's God.

> The LORD is my rock, my fortress and my deliverer;
>> my God is *my rock,* in whom I take refuge,
>> *my shield* and the horn of *my salvation.*
> He is *my stronghold, my refuge* and *my savior—*
>> from violent men you save me.
>
> —vv. 2–3, emphasis added

As the song continues, there is the history of what God has done in very descriptive terms. Over and over, God has rescued David from battles, bouts of depression, close calls with death, and from great distress.

By verse 8, David begins to describe the indescribable. David tries to paint a picture of what God is like, of what it looks like to see God in action. Try to envision everything David paints, from the earthquake to an angry, almighty God riding a cherubim through the skies. As you read the words, slow down and really envision what David describes.

> The earth trembled and quaked,
>   the foundations of the heavens shook;
>   they trembled because he was angry.
> Smoke rose from his nostrils;
>   consuming fire came from his mouth,
>   burning coals blazed out of it.
> He parted the heavens and came down;
>   dark clouds were under his feet.
> He mounted the cherubim and flew;
>   he soared on the wings of the wind.
> He made darkness his canopy around him—
>   the dark rain clouds of the sky.
> Out of the brightness of his presence
>   bolts of lightning blazed forth.
> The LORD thundered from heaven;
>   the voice of the Most High resounded.
> He shot arrows and scattered the enemies,
>   bolts of lightning and routed them.
> The valleys of the sea were exposed
>   and the foundations of the earth laid bare
>   at the rebuke of the LORD,
>   at the blast of breath from his nostrils.
>   —vv. 8–16

Wow! Did you see it? Did you really try to grasp a picture of this powerful, mighty, angry God? If you did, then get ready for a wonderful, overwhelming realization. There is a reason for why God goes to all this trouble—*and the reason is that God loves you.*

He reached down from on high and took hold of *me;*
   he drew *me* out of deep waters.
He rescued *me* from *my* powerful enemy,
   from *my* foes, who were too strong for *me.*
They confronted *me* in the day of *my* disaster,
   but the LORD was *my* support.
He brought *me* out into a spacious place;
   he rescued *me* because *he delighted in me.*
                                   —vv. 17–20, emphasis added

Now that I've thought about it, I can think of plenty of times when God has rescued me. Can you? If you live long enough, you're going to see a lot of enemies. No, not the person who gives you an obscene gesture when he cuts in front of you in city traffic— *real* enemies.

Perhaps your enemies are real people. More than likely, your enemies might be grief, despair, and depression. Enemies like disease and pain. Enemies like financial pressure or family struggles. Enemies like mistakes from the past that continually haunt you. Enemies that life throws at you without the least provocation, without the least bit of warning. Like the Philistines attacking old David, they'll attack you when you're at your weakest, most vulnerable points. But know the truth: In the midst of those great battles of life, God is faithful to the faithful. For those who will look to Him, and not at circumstances, there is joy in the midst of hardship, confidence in the midst of defeat, praise in the midst of great pain.

There is the startling revelation that will hit you just when you least expect it: Your Father loves you. He loves to love you. He delights in you. But this truth is even more overwhelming than simply knowing that God loves you: God loves you despite your shortcomings.

The Love Is Unconditional

If you didn't know the life of David, you might read the next verses and never realize that the singer of the song had ever committed a sin, that he had ever been guilty of murder, of adultery, of gross lying, of cover-up schemes. You'd never know that he hadn't been the ideal father. Listen to the man with a song on his heart.

> The LORD has dealt with me *according to my* righteousness;
>   according to the cleanness of my hands he has rewarded
>   me.
> For I have kept the ways of the LORD;
>   I have not done evil by turning from my God.
> All his laws are before me;
>   I have not turned away from his decrees.
> I have been blameless before him
>   and have kept myself from sin.
> The LORD has rewarded me according to my righteousness,
>   according to my cleanness in his sight.
>
> To the faithful you show yourself faithful,
>   to the blameless you show yourself blameless,
> to the pure you show yourself pure,
>   but to the crooked you show yourself shrewd.
> You save the humble,
>   but your eyes are on the haughty to bring them low.
>   —vv. 21–28, emphasis added

Righteousness? Cleanness of hands? Blameless? What in the world is David thinking? Has he had a stroke, a sudden loss of memory? Surely he still walks past the graves of a baby, of Amnon, of Absalom, all dead as an indirect result of his sins. Has he never walked past Tamar's room, heard her soft crying, and remembered again that she's never married, never trusted another man, never held her own baby because of Amnon's sin, because of her own father's example? Surely, as he looks in Bathsheba's eyes, he sometimes sees a weary hollowness that wasn't there on the sparkling-eye night of their one-day fling. Had he never introduced himself, she would be happily married to her husband Uriah.

Surely he reads the newspaper headlines of a country divided over his own leadership skills.

Why can't he remember his own sins? How can he lift one foot and put it in front of another? Isn't it dark in David's life? If you've ever struggled with your own sin, keep reading, for David was right in the way he felt. His joy was well founded!

> You are my lamp, O LORD;
>> the LORD turns my darkness into light.
> With your help I can advance against a troop;
>> with my God I can scale a wall.
>
> As for God, his way is perfect;
>> the word of the LORD is flawless.
> He is a shield
>> for all who take refuge in him.
> For who is God besides the LORD?
>> And who is the Rock except our God?
> *It is God who arms me with strength*
>> *and makes my way perfect.*
> He makes my feet like the feet of a deer;
>> he enables me to stand on the heights.
>> —vv. 29–34, emphasis added

The greatest miracle and the greatest victory you will experience in life is feeling God's forgiveness. To be aware that a holy God holds your sins against you no more is an awesome thought. But to honestly be set free of the chains of guilt, to be able to sing a song of praise in your old age, after ages of doing wrong—what an exhilarating feeling! What an incredible thing it is to be able to sing at all. What a joy it is to have a light heart. No wonder we'll sing such incredible songs in heaven, where we'll know God's great forgiveness. But you can, like David, discover the song in your heart today! Searching for God's heart will, my friend, give you a light heart. Finding that the relationship with God is achieved even through the searching process will give you feet as light as the deer leaping across mountain paths.

Why don't most Christians take up God's offer for joy? Bill Chitwood tells the story of an old gentleman who had gone to the store to buy a bag of potatoes. On his way home, a man picked him up and gave him a ride. The old gentleman sat on the front seat of the car holding the bag of potatoes on his lap. After some time, the driver said, "Why don't you put those potatoes down in the floorboard? There's no need for you to hold them in your lap. They must be heavy." The old gentleman replied, "Oh, I wouldn't think of doing that. You were good enough to give me a ride, the least I can do is carry these potatoes."

Since God has forgiven you of your sins, is there any reason for you to carry that bag of potatoes, that heavy bag of guilt, anymore? Let it go. Give it up. Rest in God's grace. God loves you, even delights in you, despite your shortcomings.

As you sing a song of joy, remember that there is something you can do to make God delight in you even more. God loves hearing the praise of a righteous life.

The Praise of a Righteous Life

Never hear a song like David's, never hear the teachings on grace, and believe the heresy that because of God's grace, *anything* we want to do is acceptable. Of course it's not. What God desires to see in our lives is praise. And praise doesn't come simply on Sunday mornings in church services. Praise comes from the way we live our lives, Monday through Saturday, and Sunday on top of that.

Remember the woman caught in adultery (see John 8)? Suddenly, just as suddenly as you and I can be caught in sin, she is nakedly exposed before her community and before Christ. She was having a sexual getaway with a man not her husband. And the man isn't there.

Sin has left her all alone, completely guilty, without a prayer for her defense. She's in more trouble than she ever imagined possible, dragged through her community, nakedly exposed. Sin does that to us.

And yet, Jesus defends her. All have sinned, all are guilty. The writing on the ground in that great story is as hidden as the writing on your heart and the writing on mine. God has a way of making our sins quite legible, and none of us is without sin. But do you remember the words of Jesus as he and the woman are eye to eye, after the crowd has gone?

> Jesus straightened up and asked her, "Woman, where are they? Has no one condemned you?"
> "No one, sir," she said.
> "Then neither do I condemn you," Jesus declared. "Go now and leave your life of sin."
> —John 8:10–11

After she left, the woman had an opportunity to live a righteous life, to no longer live in sin. If she did, God was praised. God was overjoyed. And she found joy, too.

The next verse records the first words Jesus spoke to a crowd perhaps that same afternoon. Surely, the sin of the woman—or was it my sin?—was still on his mind.

> When Jesus spoke again to the people, he said, "I am the light of the world. Whoever follows me will never walk in darkness, but will have the light of life."
> —John 8:12

David knew that God expected him to live in a righteous manner, to praise Him with all his heart and all of his actions. After his lowest moment, David never again, according to the record in the Bible, committed an act of lust or an act of adultery. He paid the consequences—the terrible consequences—of the bed he had made, and he moved on. He learned about God's love, about God's forgiveness, and then *he lived like it made a difference to be forgiven.* Yes, there is this song of David's heart in 2 Samuel 22, but the real song was in his life, a life lived in a righteous manner.

The LORD lives! Praise be to my Rock!
    Exalted be God, the Rock, my Savior!
He is the God who avenges me,
    who puts the nations under me,
    who sets me free from my enemies.
You exalted me above my foes;
    from violent men you rescued me.
Therefore I will praise you, O LORD, among the nations;
    I will sing praises to your name.
He gives his king great victories;
    he shows unfailing kindness to his anointed,
    to David and his descendants forever.

—vv. 47–51

Have you accepted the forgiveness of God—really, honestly, securely felt the freedom of knowing that God holds your sin against you no more? He doesn't. Because of the sacrifice of His Son, Jesus Christ, God can freely give forgiveness to all who desire it. Jesus was without sin, and when He died on the cross, the world wasn't just seeing an execution. The world was seeing the greatest act of substitution ever created. It was your sin, my sin, that caused the death of Jesus Christ, and He willingly died for us. He fought the battle with Satan over our sin as surely as God rescued David from his warring enemies.

Having faith in a loving, forgiving God, David was secure in God's love three thousand years ago. Even after all he had done, he was secure. He was forgiven. Are you secure in God's love today?

And one more question: Are you living your life as if it has made a difference to be forgiven? God doesn't just give us the power to be forgiven. God gives us the power to walk away from sin. After all, says the Bible, "No temptation has seized you except what is common to man. And God is faithful; he will not let you be tempted beyond what you can bear. But when you are tempted, he will also provide a way out so that you can stand up under it" (1 Cor. 10:13).

When you walk away from temptation, you are in the process of praising God, of living a righteous life! And that is the song from your heart that God loves to hear.

The Masterpiece in You

In the pages of this book, we've spent a lot of time remembering David. Perhaps you've envisioned the work of Michelangelo Buonarroti, the masterful artist and sculptor who lived in the sixteenth century. One of his most famous works—indeed, one of the most famous works of art in all the world—stands in Florence, Italy.

Nearly eighteen feet of finely crafted stone bring to life the colossal figure of David. Millions have seen it, and millions have recognized it as a great masterpiece. Some would call it Michelangelo's greatest work.

Want to know a bit of great irony? The stone from which Michelangelo chiseled away the young king was a reject. The huge piece of marble had been rejected by other great artists of his day. The stone, they all saw, was flawed. Michelangelo saw that the stone was flawed, too. You couldn't help but see the flaw. It was as easily seen as the flaw in your own life, as easily seen as the flaw in my life. But it was from this flawed, rejected stone that Michelangelo's great work emerged.

Listen to me. Maybe other people don't know about the flaw in your life, but *you know it's there*. And God knows it's there. You and God have seen the worst side of your life, the flaw that makes the marble of you a reject. But wait a moment! Here is great, great news. God still loves you, and God is ready, willing, and able to make a masterpiece out of your life, despite your shortcomings.

Want to be a man, a woman, a boy, a girl, a teenager after God's own heart? Invite God to get out His chisel and start, or continue, the long, slow process of bringing a masterpiece out of your life. God sees your potential, God loves you, and God wants to show the world what He can do with you.

Never settle for a religion, never settle for tradition. Accept only a real relationship with the living God through a living Savior, Jesus Christ. And as you go about the search, may you, too, be called a person after God's own heart.

Notes

Acknowledgments
1. Beth Moore, *A Heart Like His: Seeking the Heart of God Through a Study of David* (Nashville: Lifeway Press, 1996).
2. Charles Swindoll, *David* (Nashville: Word, 1997).

Chapter 4
1. According to Lifeway Christian Resources's Tom Carringer, a 1990 Constituency Study of 1,779 Southern Baptist adults, 20 percent of the nearly sixteen-million member denomination (3.2 million) had not attended church at all during the previous six months, and another 15 percent (2.4 million) had attended once a month or less during the previous six months.
2. Wesley Taylor, conversation with author, 11 September 1998.

Chapter 5
1. Ed Grisamore, *True Gris: The Best of Ed Grisamore* (Macon, Ga.: Mercer University Press, 1997), 24–26.

Chapter 8

1. Barney Kasdan, *God's Appointed Customs: A Messianic Jewish Guide to the Biblical Lifecycle and Lifestyle* (Baltimore: Lederer Messianic, 1984), 124.

Chapter 12

1. Chuck Yeager and Leo Janas, *Yeager* (New York: Bantam Books, 1985), 176.

2. Robert Hastings, *A Penny's Worth of Minced Ham: Another Look at the Great Depression* (Carbondale, Ill.: Southern Illinois University Press, 1986).

3. Beth Moore, *A Heart Like His: Seeking the Heart of God Through a Study of David* (Nashville: Lifeway Press, 1996), 118.

Chapter 13

1. M. Douglas Ivester, Chairman, Board of Directors and CEO, at Coca-Cola's web page (www.coca-cola.com), 11 September 1998.

2. Patrick J. Carnes, *Don't Call It Love* (New York: Bantam Books, 1991), 57.